LEGAL AND POLITICAL HERMENEUTICS,

OR PRINCIPLES

OF INTERPRETATION AND CONSTRUCTION

IN LAW AND POLITICS,

WITH REMARKS

ON PRECEDENTS AND AUTHORITIES.

ENLARGED EDITION.

BY FRANCIS LIEBER.

THE LAWBOOK EXCHANGE, LTD.
Clark, New Jersey

ISBN-13: 9781584772262 (hardcover)
ISBN-13: 9781616190293 (paperback)

Lawbook Exchange edition 2002, 2010

The quality of this reprint is equivalent to the quality of the original work.

THE LAWBOOK EXCHANGE, LTD.
33 Terminal Avenue
Clark, New Jersey 07066-1321

Please see our website for a selection of our other publications and fine facsimile reprints of classic works of legal history:
www.lawbookexchange.com

Library of Congress Cataloging-in-Publication Data

Lieber, Francis, 1800-1872.
  Legal and political hermeneutics, or, Principles of interpretation and construction in law
  and politics : with remarks on precedents and authorities / by Francis Lieber.—Enl. ed.
        p. cm.
    Originally published: Boston: C.C. Little and J. Brown, 1839.
    Includes index.
    ISBN 1-58477-226-3 (cloth: alk. paper)
    1. Law—Interpretation and construction. 2. Law—Language. 3. Semantics (Law) 4.   Political science—Methodology. I. Title: Legal and political hermeneutics. II. Title:
  Principles of interpretation and construction in law and politics.
  III. Title.

    K290 .L54 2002
    340'. 1'4—dc21
                                                                2002024218

Printed in the United States of America on acid-free paper

LEGAL AND POLITICAL HERMENEUTICS,

OR PRINCIPLES

OF INTERPRETATION AND CONSTRUCTION

IN LAW AND POLITICS,

WITH REMARKS

ON PRECEDENTS AND AUTHORITIES.

ENLARGED EDITION.

BY FRANCIS LIEBER.

BOSTON:
CHARLES C. LITTLE AND JAMES BROWN.
MDCCCXXXIX.

TO THE HONORABLE

JAMES KENT, LL. D.,

RESPECTFULLY INSCRIBED,

BY THE AUTHOR.

S. N. Dickinson, Printer.

Entered according to Act of Congress, in the year 1839, by
Francis Lieber,
In the Clerk's Office of the District Court of the District of Massachusetts.

Dear Sir,

Your name placed at the head of so small a work, may appear, to many readers, not unlike a noble front of granite, which hides but a common brick building, and deceives the unobserving passer-by. But the very fact that I was bold enough to grace so insignificant a book with your name, must plead for me; for it will show, at least, how anxious I was to express my deep respect for your labors, and my sincere thanks for your indulgence towards mine. May the additions I have made to the Hermeneutics not induce you to change the opinion which you were kindly disposed to take of the first edition.

   I am,
    Dear Sir,
     Your respectful servant,
      FRANCIS LIEBER.

PREFACE.

One of the first articles, which I read after my landing at New York, now nearly twelve years ago, was in a paper opposed to the administration of Mr. Adams. The construction of the constitution formed one of the points on which the writer founded his objections to the president and his party. The subject, as a distinction of political men and measures, was new to me, as political construction in this aspect, is peculiarly American; for, here, the idea of written constitutions, of which it is a consequence, was first realized permanently and on a large scale, although they have existed at earlier dates. My attention was naturally attracted by this subject, and the more attention I paid to the whole political system, in which I have lived ever since, the more important it appeared to me, not, indeed, as a matter of curiosity, but one which involves the gravest interests of right. When, however, the idea of trying to reduce upon ethic principles that which yet appears so unsettled in

PREFACE. vii

practical municipal politics, and to find some firm and solid foundations of right and morality, in the rolling tides of party actions, was gradually matured in my mind; when I finally concluded to undertake a work on Political Ethics, I was naturally led to reflect more thoroughly on Construction, and to arrange my thoughts in systematic order. For it seems evident that mathematics alone can wholly dispense with interpretation and construction of some sort, while, on the other hand, without good faith they become desperate weapons in the hands of the disingenuous. They form, therefore, a subject which clearly appertains to legal and political morals. But when I came to write down my observations in their proper connexion, I found that they extended much beyond the limits which could be fairly allowed to a single chapter, nor did the crowd of subjects admit of more than one being occupied by this specific one. They were published in the American Jurist,* after which I thought I might, perhaps, succeed in pruning them to a more proportionate size for the then projected and now half published work. I was told, however, that the article had found favor with the readers of the Jurist, and that a reduction would materially injure it, while I was called upon by several professional gentlemen of eminence, to publish the article separately. I followed their advice, the more readily as I was desirous of

---

* October number of 1837, and January number of 1838.

adding some remarks, which appear to me of sufficient importance, to enlarge the chapter on precedents, and to add a new one on authorities. I have re-written the whole, as a superficial comparison will show, and here lay the result of my labors before the reader. May it do some good. Whether I have succeeded or not, I believe it will be granted on all hands, that the subject is a very important one, and that in countries, as the United States and England, in which civil liberty teaches the citizen to look for one of its great protections in the exact administration of the laws, and a careful avoidance of constant explanation, not interpretation, of the laws by the Public Power— in countries, in which the law is allowed to make its own way, immutable principles and fixed rules for interpreting and construing them, should be generally acknowledged, or if they exist already, in a scattered state, should be gathered and clearly represented, so that they may establish themselves along with the laws, as part and branch of the common law of free countries.

January 1, 1839.

CONTENTS.

CHAPTER I.

No direct communion between the Minds of Men; Signs are necessary.—What Signs are.—Utterance.—Various Signs used to convey Ideas.—Interpretation; its definition.—Etymology of the word.—Interpretation is not arbitrary, but ought to proceed by rules.—Words; what they are.—Words most common Signs of Communion between Men.—Interpretation of Words.—Text.—Utterer..................13

CHAPTER II.

Ambiguity of Human Speech.—Processes of Formation of Words.—Necessity of always leaving much to be understood by Interpretation.—Not to be avoided by Specification and Amplification.—Causes of Ambiguity in the Language, the Utterer, the Change of Circumstances.—Desire of avoiding different Interpretation.—Prohibition of Commentaries.—Napoleon's View.—Interpretation cannot be dispensed with.—Civil Liberty demands Independence of the Judiciary, of the Law.—Correct Interpretation more necessary in free Countries than in States not free..................25

CHAPTER III.

Construction.—Its Definition.—Twofold Application of this Definition.—Necessity of Construction, when Interpretation ceases to avail.—Necessity of distinguishing between Interpretation and Construction.—Instance.—Doctrine of Cy-pres. Science of Hermeneutics.—Derivation of the word.—Construction, although dangerous, yet indispensable.—Different Species of Interpretation, to arrive at the True Sense.—Close Interpretation.—Literal Interpretation is an inadmissible Term.—Instances of pretended Literal Interpretation.—Extensive Interpretation.—Liberal Interpretation not a good Term.—Extravagant Interpretation.—Limited and Free Interpretation.—Predestined Interpretation.—Artful Interpretation.—Authentic Interpretation.—Different Species of Theologic Interpretation.—Close, Comprehensive, Transcendant, Extravagant Construction.—Indemnity Bills............55

CHAPTER IV.

Principles of sound Interpretation.— Genuineness of the Text. Falsified Texts in the highest as the lowest Spheres.—No Sentence of Words can have more than one True Sense. — Double Interpretation is false Interpretation. — Good Faith and Common Sense the leading Stars of all Genuine Interpretation. — Moral Obligation of Legal Counsel. — Lord Brougham's Opinion. — What Good Faith is in Interpretation. — Peculiar Circumstances which may make Subterfuges laudable. — Literal Interpretation an ever ready means of Tyranny.— Political Shuffling. — Words to be taken in their most probable sense.— Usus Loquendi. — To what it may relate. — Rules to ascertain the Meaning of doubtful Words.— ' Contemporanea expositio est fortissima in Lege.' — Instances. Technical Terms to be taken in their technical sense.—That which is inferior cannot defeat that which is superior. — The Text itself must furnish, if possible, the means of interpreting its own doubtful Words. — High Considerations on account of which we have to abandon Interpretation. — Case of Lord Bentink's Order in Council, abolishing Whipping of native Indian Soldiers, and a Sepoy and Drummer being lashed, because, having become a Christian, he was not entitled to the Privilege of Natives. — Care of Sir Thomas Parkyns. — Recapitulation of the Principles of Interpretation.........83

CHAPTER V.

Construction is unavoidable.— The Causes why.—Instances.— Analogy or Parallelism the main Guide in Construing.—Rules of Construing. — We begin with that which is near. — Aim and Object of the Text. — Preambles of Laws. — Shall the Motives of the Utterer guide us? — How far?—'Lex Neminem cogit ad Impossibilia.'— Texts conferring Privileges. — Close construction necessary in construing Contracts. — Construction of Promises and Obligations. — Maximum and Minimum. — That which agrees most with the Spirit and Tenor of the Text is preferable. — Effects and Consequences of the Construction may guide us.— Blackstone.—Antiquity of Law makes frequently extensive Construction necessary. — Habitual close Interpretation and Construction favorable to Civil Liberty.— Words of a relative or generic Meaning to be taken in a relative or expansive Sense. — Rules respecting this Point.—The Weak have the Benefit of Doubt. — The Superior Object cannot be defeated by the Inferior. — Recapitulation of the Principles of Construction................121

CHAPTER VI.

Hermeneutic Rules respecting Detached spoken Words or Sentences. — Conversation. — Hearsay. — In judicial Procedures. Letters, Journals, Private Notes. — Speeches. — Pamphlets.— Orders, Directions, &c. of a passing Nature. — Contracts, Deeds, Wills, &c.— Laws must at times be interpreted or construed. — Hermeneutic Rules respecting Laws. — Constitutions. — Constitutions are Laws and Guarantees. — Various Constitutions. — Rules of Constitutional Hermeneutics.—The Veto and pardoning Privilege. — International Treaties...145

CHAPTER VII.

Precedents.—Definition.—Natural Power of Precedents.—Power of Precedent in England.—Reasons of the Powerful Influence of Precedents.—' Wisdom of our Forefathers.'—Lineal Assent, Contemporary Assent.—Great Force, for Good or Evil, of Precedents in Politics.—Reasons.—Distinction between Legal and Political Precedents.—Precedents of a mixed Character.—Precedents necessary for the Development of Law for Civil Liberty.—They settle the Knowledge of what is Law.—Necessary Qualities of sound Legal Precedents.—Executive Acts are no Precedents, except for subordinate Officers if not against Law.—Fearful Instance of Executive Precedent in the History of the Star Chamber.—No Man shall take advantage of his own Wrong.—Sound Precedents.—Precedents must be taken with all their Adjuncts.—No Precedent weighs against Law and Right.—Still less against Reason.—Precedents must not increase Public Power.—Precedents must settle, not unsettle.—Precedents may be overruled if necessary. The greatest Lawyers have done so, for instance, Lord Coke. 192

CHAPTER VIII.

Authorities.—Akin to Precedents.—Definition.—Ought we to submit to them?—Slavish Submission to them; Arrant Disregard of them.—We must always adopt Authorities in many Branches.—Main Questions of Historic Criticism.—Similar ones regarding Authorities.—Who is he?—What opportunity had he to know the Subject?—What Motive prompted him? What internal Evidence is there?—Of what Extent is the Authority?—Various Phases of the same Authority.—Classical Periods..223

CHAPTER I.

No direct communion between the Minds of Men; Signs are necessary. — What Signs are. — Utterance. — Various Signs used to convey Ideas. — Interpretation; its definition. — Etymology of the word. Interpretation is not arbitrary, but ought to proceed by rules.—Words; what they are. — Words most common Signs of Communion between Men. — Interpretation of Words. — Text. — Utterer.

I. There is no direct communion between the minds of men; whatever thoughts, emotions, conceptions, ideas of delight or sufferance we feel urged to impart to other individuals, we cannot obtain our object without resorting to the outward manifestation of that which moves us inwardly, that is, to signs. There is no immediate communion between the minds of individuals, as long as we are on this earth, without signs, that is, expressions perceptible by the senses. The most thrilling emotions of a mother's heart, watching over a suffering child, the most abstract meditation of the philosopher, the sublimest conception of the poet, or the most faithful devotion of a martyr in a pure and noble cause, can no more be perceived by others or communicated to them without signs or manifestations, than the most common desires of daily intercourse, or our physical wants for sustenance or protection.

II. Signs, in this most comprehensive sense, would include all manifestations of the inward man, and extend as well to the deeds performed by an individual, inasmuch as they enable us to understand his plans and motives, as to those signs used for the sole purpose of expressing some ideas; in other words, the term would include all marks, intentional or unintentional, by which one individual may understand the mind or the whole disposition of another, as well as those which express a single idea or emotion; for instance, the look of tenderness or tear of compassion, as well as the mile stone on the road, or the skull and cross bones painted on a vessel which contains deadly poison.

There is a primeval principle in man, which ever urges him with irresistible power to represent outwardly what moves him strongly within, a pressing urgency of utterance, so that men, through all the many spheres of life and action, feel a want of manifesting without, that which stirs their mind or heart, even though there be no direct object which they consciously desire to obtain by this manifestation. The anxious desire of utterance is independent of any principle of utility, that is, of the conscious desire of obtaining a certain end by the manifestation of our inward state. A victory is gained; the people rejoice at it; they illuminate their houses, and light bonfires. It may be far in the interior, at a great distance from the enemy. They neither do it, to taunt the hostile armies, nor peculiarly to honor the victors. They do it, because their minds and souls are in a state of triumph and rejoicing, and they cannot resist expressing it. A temple is to be built for the reception of those who feel a wish to adore their God. The building is planned and executed in a nobler style than the ordinary dwellings of men, not to flatter the deity or to honor the Most High, for the fabric may be building by those whose religion teaches them that He cannot be flattered by men, that his honor does not depend upon frail mortals, but because their mind, in erecting a church is in a different frame from what it is, when they build a cottage, and they feel urged to manifest it accordingly. Man dresses differently for a gay feast, than for a funeral of his departed friend. Man might sleep on straw as his domestic animals do, and soundly and healthily too, but he has an innate love of the beautiful, and it urges him to surround himself with tasteful furniture, even, not unfrequently against the dictates of mere utility; although I would observe, passingly, that this innate love of the beautiful, which in some stage of development, we find with all men, and with no animal, is one of the broad foundations of all industry, but not consciously made so by reflecting utilitarianism or, as it is termed by others, enlightened self-interest; another mind, and a deeper wisdom than human intellect is capable of, has made this one of the first and indestructible foundations of civilization.

One more remark respecting this subject, and I shall turn to what more directly occupies us. I have endeavored, in another work,[1] to show how indispensably man's individuality is connected with his morality. Had the Creator established a means of direct influence of mind upon mind among men, such for instance as the adherents to the theory of animal magnetism pretend to have found, it would seem that this individuality would be greatly impaired, perhaps totally destroyed. Yet it was the evident plan of our Maker, to link man to man, to lead him to society, and lead this society from stage to stage. Absolute individuality or utterance restricted for the purpose of utility, would have fettered man in the lowest bondage of sordid

(1) Political Ethics, vol. 1, book 1.

egotism; and God may have impressed that urgency of manifestation indelibly upon the human soul, as one of the chiefest means of sociability, civilization and elevation. For nearly all that is choicest in mankind is owing first of all to this irresistible anxiety of manifestation.

III. The signs which man uses, the using of which implies intention, for the purpose of conveying ideas or notions to his fellow-creatures, are very various, for instance, gestures, signals, telegraphs, monuments, sculptures of all kinds, pictorial and hieroglyphic signs, the stamp on coins, seals, beacons, buoys, insignia, ejaculations, articulate sounds, or their representations, that is phonetic characters on stones, wood, leaves, paper, &c., entire periods, or single words, such as names in a particular place, and whatever other signs, even the flowers in the flower language of the East, might be enumerated.

IV. These signs then are used to convey certain ideas, and interpretation, in its widest meaning, is the discovery and representation of the true meaning of any signs, used to convey ideas.

The 'true meaning' of any signs is that meaning which those who used them were desirous of expressing. (See sect. vii.)

'Using signs' does not only signify the origination of their combination in a given case, but also the declared or well understood adoption or sanction of them, wherever there are several parties, who endeavor to express their ideas by the same combination of signs.

In the case of a compact, for instance, treaty, contract, or any act of the nature of an agreement, the party, who avowedly adopts the contract, treaty, &c., or gives his tacit assent to it, makes as much use of the signs declaratory of the agreement, as the party who originated them. Forced silence, or the impossibility of expressing dissent, is, of course not comprehended within the term 'tacit assent.' The ancient rule in law, therefore, that: 'qui tacet consentire videtur,' is correct, provided we give the proper meaning to the term 'videtur.' It has been justly amplified thus: 'Qui tacet verbo et facto, ubi obloqui vel resistere potest ac debet, consentire videtur.'[1] If a person is deceived, his silence is of course not consent, nor is it such if he that has power, first prohibits all contradiction, and afterwards construes silence into assent, a case which has repeatedly occurred in history.

(1) Krug, Professor of Philosophy in the University at Leipzig, in his Philosophy of Law, (Rechtslehre.)

V. All the signs, enumerated in section iv. require interpretation, that is, it is necessary for him, for whose benefit they are intended, to find out, what those persons who used the sign, intend to convey to the mind of the beholder or hearer. Thus, some beacons signify to the approaching mariner that there is great danger in their vicinity; others indicate, by their guiding light, the safest passage into a port. If the mariner does not know how to interpret these signs, he will attach a wrong meaning to them, or be at a loss what meaning they have. Thus, likewise, have the historian and antiquarian to interpret inscriptions on medals, and not only the words they may contain, but also certain emblems, representations of animals or things. Pictures must be likewise interpreted, for instance, those which are found on the walls of Egyptian temples; that is to say, it is one of the occupations of the historian and antiquarian to find out the meaning of these various representations, i. e. the ideas which he who made them (or ordered them to be made) intended to convey to the beholder.

If we believe that one of the objects of God, in creating the world, was to manifest his wisdom and goodness to man, the expression of interpreting nature is correct. By interpreting the actions of a man,[1] we mean to designate the endeavor to arrive at their direct meaning, the motives from which they flowed, by construing his actions, we rather indicate an endeavor of arriving at conclusions with reference to the whole character of the acting individual or at least at something, which lies beyond the nearest motives of the specific acts in question. This agrees substantially with the difference between interpretation and construction, which will appear in the course of this work.[2]

(1) To *explain* and *interpret*, are not confined to what is written or said, they are employed likewise with regard to the actions of men.' Crabb Eng. Syn., ad verb. *Explain*.

(2) It is always well to have everything as clear around us, as possible; it gives light and imparts vigor to the mind, if we see the Whence and Whither of things, and trace connection where insulation seems to exist; even though it be in matters apparently trifling. I hope to be pardoned therefore, by the strictly practical Lawyer, if I dwell for a moment on the origin of the word, which claims our attention for the present, in a sphere, very different from that of Law.

To Interpret, as is well known, is derived from the Latin *interpres, interpretari*, a compound of *inter* and *pretari*. The latter belongs, as nearly all truly Latin words, according to its root, to that language, which was spoken by the original inhabitants or settlers of Europe, and of which the Gothic, Ancient High German, Swedish, Icelandic, Latin &c., are but descended, and which was likewise either the first foundation of the Greek, or so strongly influenced it, that the root of enumerable words is easily traced through all these languages. The many profound inquiries of European philologists have brought so many facts to light, that this connection may be considered as firmly established, while historic inquiries have shown the vast population of Italy long before any records of the Romans began.

Pretari is of the same root with many words in Teutonic languages; *prata* in Swedish is speaking; we have *prating* and *prattling*; the German *reden* (pronounce *raden*,) speaking, is the

VI. The idea, involved in the term Interpretation, that we have to discover the true meaning of signs, and represent it to others, implies, likewise, that we proceed in doing so, on safe ground, according to rules established by reason, and not arbitrarily or whimsically. On this account, interpretation, and, as will be seen in the sequel, construction, are distinct from conjecture. Still it lies in the nature of things, that, in some cases, they approach to each other.

Conjecture is vague, interpretation is distinct; but in as far as that, which is to be interpreted, affords less and less opportunity for the application of the rules established for interpretation, the latter approaches to conjecture; provided we have not to apply construction.

VII. Those signs, by which man most frequently endeavors to convey his ideas to another, and by which in most cases he best succeeds in conveying them, are words.

---

same, for *d* and *t* easily change, while a consonant before another (*P* in this case,) is frequently dropped, or it may be that *reden* is the original. *Präten* signifies, to this day, in some parts of Germany, speaking loud and monotonously. *Prædicare* and the Greek φράζειν belong to the same family of words. It is very possible that *pretari* and *prating* are of the same root with *broad*, German *breit*, speak broadly, plainly.—The present German word for interpreting is *auslegen*, laying out, laying open, unfolding.

Words are articulate sounds, or the representation of them on or in some material, by certain adopted characters, to which, single or combined, we attach certain fixed ideas. The idea or notion thus attached to any word is called its signification; the general idea, or the assemblage of ideas or notions, conveyed by several words grammatically connected together, is called the sense or meaning of the words or period. The true sense or meaning is that which they ought to convey.

It is clear, therefore, that the term, true sense, in its most comprehensive adaptation, may signify different things, according to the different object we have in view. Thus a teacher will say to his pupil, who has unskilfully expressed himself: 'you meant to say such a thing, but the true meaning of your period is quite a different one; that is, the meaning which your words express, according to their signification, and the rules of combining them, universally adopted, is different from what you intended to say.' The teacher is right in calling the true sense, that which the words express according to the general rules, for his object is to teach the pupil how to convey his ideas correctly and perspicuously, to make use, therefore, of the words according to rules generally adopted, without which there would be no such thing as understanding one another among

CHAPTER I. — SECTION VIII. 23

men. The case changes, however, when the object of the speaker or writer is, not to learn the use of words, but simply to convey certain ideas. True sense is in this case the meaning which the person or persons, who made use of the words, intended to convey to others, whether he used them correctly, skilfully, logically or not.

Understanding or comprehending a speaker or something written, means attaching the same signification or sense to the words which the speaker or writer intended to convey.

VIII. Inasmuch, therefore, as the term interpretation is applied to words, used as the common means of converse or communion among men, we define it thus:

Interpretation is the art of finding out the true sense of any form of words: that is, the sense which their author intended to convey, and of enabling others to derive from them the same idea which the author intended to convey. It was this latter which was meant by the word 'representation' in section iv. of this chapter.

Sometimes interpretation signifies, likewise, the art which teaches us the principles, according to which we ought to proceed in order to find the true sense. See Prolegomena iii. in Ernesti, Institutio

Interpretis, page 6, vol. I. in the translation of Mr. Terrot, vol. I. of the Biblical Cabinet, Edinburgh, 1832. This art or science, however, is better called the principles of interpretation, or, which is preferable to either, hermeneutics, of which more will be said hereafter.

IX. In law and politics we have to deal so little with the interpretation of any other signs than words, that the term Interpretation, if used without any additional expression, means always the interpretation of words.

For the sake of brevity, the term Text will be used, to designate the word or words, or discourse to be interpreted or construed, or the whole writing in which they are contained. The term Utterer will be used for the author of the words to be interpreted, whether he uttered them in writing, or orally.

CHAPTER II.

Ambiguity of Human Speech.—Processes of Formation of Words.—Necessity of always leaving much to be understood by Interpretation.—Not to be avoided by Specification and Amplification.—Causes of Ambiguity in the Language, the Utterer, the Change of Circumstances.—Desire of avoiding different Interpretation.— Prohibition of Commentaries.—Napoleon's View.—Interpretation cannot be dispensed with.—Civil Liberty demands Independence of the Judiciary, of the Law.—Correct Interpretation more necessary in free Countries than in States not free.

I. If Interpretation is the discovery of the true sense of words, it is presumed that this sense is not obvious; for, that which must be discovered or found out, must needs be hidden in some way or other before it is discovered. Yet words signify ideas or things, and how does it happen, that, if used for the very purpose of conveying our ideas, they can leave any doubt?

The ambiguity of human speech is owing to a vast variety of causes, at times intentional, at others unintentional, avoidable or unavoidable, owing to the utterer, to the words or the situation of things and their changes. The most common or most important causes will be given here, and it is necessary to weigh them well, since many errors in the highest spheres of politics and law have arisen from an insufficient consideration of these causes, and a consequent belief, which still manifests itself not unfrequently in many, that ambiguity can be entirely avoided, or that certain instruments of the gravest import do not contain any, and, consequently do not require interpretation.

II. In no case are words, originally, produced in a finished state by the reflecting intellect, and consciously affixed to objects, presenting themselves to the mind in their clearly defined state, but on the contrary, things, actions (rather *activities*,) in short, phenomena, present themselves as a whole, with a number of adjuncts, a mass of adhesion, and become in the course of time only, enlarged in their meaning to more generic terms, or a prominent quality strikes so manifestly the human mind, that it alone urges to utterance, which in course of time only becomes more restricted to specific objects. As, however, these processes are going on, at the same time, with many people, subject indeed to the same general laws, but not being under the same specific influences, the natural consequence is, that terms receive a meaning, distinct indeed as to some points, but indistinct as to others, or, to use a simile, they may be distinct as to the central point of the space they cover, but become less so the farther we remove from that centre, somewhat like certain territories of civilized people bordering on wild regions. This, then, would be a necessary cause of ambiguity, even if the nature of things and ideas itself were not so that mathematical precision becomes impossible, except in mathematics themselves.

III. Were we desirous, therefore, of avoiding every possible doubt, as to what we say, even in the most common concerns of our daily life, even if we pronounce so simple a sentence as 'give me some bread,' endless explanations and specifications would be necessary; but in far the greater number of cases, the difficulties would only increase, since one specification would require another. To be brief, the very nature and essence of human language, being as we have seen, not a direct communion of minds, but a communion by intermediate signs only, renders a total exclusion of every imaginable misapprehension, in most cases, absolutely impossible.

There are some nursery stories, representing, to the great amusement of the little ones, people who are prompted by a pedantic anxiety to speak with absolute clearness, and only entangle themselves in endless explanations, one upon the other, until the whole story ends with an utter inability of the pedant to ask for the commonest thing, and he dies of hunger. These stories are founded upon the principles touched upon above, and though but nursery tales, they contain a truth, which for a long time was little acknowledged in the drawing up of laws, wherein, it was believed, explanation and specification, piled upon explanation, would produce greater and greater clearness, while in fact they produced greater and greater obscurity.

IV. Let us take an instance of the simplest kind, to show in what degree we are continually obliged to resort to interpretation. By and by we shall find that the same rules which common sense teaches every one to use, in order to understand his neighbor in the most trivial intercourse, are necessary likewise, although not sufficient, for the interpretation of documents or texts of the highest importance, constitutions as well as treaties between the greatest nations.

Suppose a housekeeper says to a domestic: 'fetch some soupmeat,' accompanying the act with giving some money to the latter, he will be unable to exe-

CHAPTER II.—SECTION IV. 29

cute the order without interpretation, however easy, and, consequently, rapid the performance of the process may be. Common sense and good faith tell the domestic, that the housekeeper's meaning was this: 1. He should go immediately, or as soon as his other occupations are finished; or, if he be directed to do so in the evening, that he should go the next day at the *usual* hour; 2. that the money handed him by the housekeeper is intended to pay for the meat thus ordered, and not as a present to him; 3. that he should buy such meat and of such parts of the animal, as, to his knowledge, has commonly been used in the house he stays at, for making soups; 4. that he buy the best meat he can obtain, for a fair price; 5. that he go to that butcher who usually provides the family, with whom the domestic resides, with meat, or to some convenient stall, and not to any unnecessarily distant place; 6. that he return the rest of the money; 7. that he bring home the meat in good faith, neither adding any thing disagreeable or injurious; 8. that he fetch the meat for the use of the family and not for himself. Suppose, on the other hand, the housekeeper, afraid of being misunderstood, had mentioned these eight specifications, she would not have obtained her object, if it were to exclude all *possibility* of misunderstanding. For, the various specifications would have required new ones. Where would be the end? We are constrained, then, always, to leave a considerable part of our meaning to be found out by interpretation, which, in many cases must necessarily cause greater or less obscurity with regard to the exact meaning, which our words were intended to convey.

Experience is a plant growing as slow as confidence, which Chatham said increased so tardily. In fact, confidence grows slowly, because it depends upon experience. The British spirit of civil liberty, induced the English judges to adhere strictly to the law, to its exact expressions. This again induced the law-makers to be, in their phraseology, as explicit and minute as possible, which causes such a tautology and endless repetition in the statutes of that country, that even so eminent a statesman as Sir Robert Peel, declared in parliament, that he ' contemplates no task with so much distaste, as the reading through an ordinary act of parliament.' Men have at length found out, that little or nothing is gained by attempting to speak with absolute clearness, and endless specifications, but that human speech is the clearer, the less we endeavor to supply by words and specifications, that interpretation which common sense must give to human words. However minutely we may define, somewhere we needs must trust at last to common sense and good faith. The words of Sir Robert Peel, introductory to his bill for amending the penal code of Great Britain, are too valuable not to find a place here. He said in the house of Commons :

'I certainly have set the example to the house, of drawing up such bills for the future, in an intelligible manner. Not being myself a lawyer, and possessing, of course, no technical knowledge, I do confess, sir, that there is no task which I contemplate with so much distaste, as the reading through an ordinary act of parliament. In the first place, the long recapitulations, the tedious references, the constant repetitions, the providing or designating offences as punishments for the specific case of men, women and children, and for every degree and relation in society, and the necessity of indicating these several personages and matters by as many appropriate relations and designations—then the confusion resulting from the attempt to describe, and constantly referring to many different descriptions of property. Really, sir, all these various repetitions, recapitulations, and references are so tedious and so perplexing, that I, for one, almost invariably find myself completely puzzled before I get to the end of a single clause. The mode I have adopted in this bill, to obviate all this confusion and uncertainty (we see, then, that the attempt at being absolutely distinct leads to greater uncertainty instead of certainty,) does seem to me, I speak it with submission, much more eligible and precise, than the usual phraseology, adopted in these acts, and might, I cannot help thinking, be pursued with advantage in bills which may be brought in hereafter.'———' Owing to the various lights in which I have considered this provision, and the extent which I have thus given to the bill, I am afraid it will be impossible to frame one more comprehensive.' So far Sir Robert.

The fact is, the English had gone, in their attempt at perfect perspicuity, so far as even to strive to exclude the interpretation of common sense, which is a matter of impossibility.

The full and redundant phraseology of Mr. Burke's will, by which he wished to pass his property to his wife and her heirs, with the codicil of July 30, 1795, is another instance of the fact, that we do not arrive at great perspicuity by going beyond a certain limit; and this limit is, where plain common sense must begin to interpret, that is, where we must begin to give to words that meaning, which, according to plain common sense, they ought to have.

The more we strive in a document to go beyond plain clearness and perspicuity, the more we do increase, in fact, the chances of sinister interpretation.

V. Words themselves, as was alluded to, may have an ambiguous signification; this arises from different causes.

1. The objects of the physical world are not so distinctly defined from each other as they appear to be at first glance. Innumerable transitions exist between them. To this day, no naturalist has yet succeeded in giving an entirely satisfactory definition of the word plant, which, as every true definition ought to do, includes the signs characteristic of all individual specimens called plants, and extends no farther, or absolutely excludes every thing else. The lawgivers of all countries have found it a difficult task to give an exact legal definition of the word arms, and one still more difficult, to define the terms defensive and offensive arms. In a criminal lawsuit one credible witness testified that he had seen a bench in a certain room covered with blood; another, equally credible, stated upon oath that he had seen, in the same room, a table and no bench, soiled with blood. The fact was, that the object sworn to, was, considered as a bench, unusually high and wide; considered as a table, low and narrow.

2. Ideas relating to the invisible world flow still more one into another; not always from want of words, but frequently on account of the gradual transitions from one extreme to another.

3. Words themselves mean different things, sometimes more, sometimes less connected with each other; or they do not signify the thing, or idea to be named, with sufficient precision. This is owing, among other reasons, to the fact, that most words expressive either of abstract ideas, or subjects belonging to the invisible world are faded tropes, that is, words meaning originally objects of the sensible world, but which are now applied to the intellectual. In many cases, therefore, different people do not connect exactly the same ideas with the same words, although they may be used everywhere.

VI. The person, who endeavors to convey some meaning to us, may not use the proper means.

1. He may be illiterate and not use the words in their most proper or generally adopted meaning.

2. He may not be sufficiently trained in grammar, to know the different signification and effect which a word acquires by a different position.

3. He may speak or write on the spur of the moment, or in great excitement, and not be able to select those means of conveying his ideas, which calm deliberation would have suggested.

4. He may be sick or dying, and not be as fully master of the means of expression, as he was in a healthy state; which is not unfrequently the case,

with regard to wills, dictated in haste, or merely pronounced in the presence of witnesses, which oral wills are valid in some countries and with certain restrictions, and are known to the common law as nuncupative wills.

VII. We may not be fully acquainted with the precise meaning, which the members of a certain sect, profession or trade, or the inhabitants of certain parts of a country may attach, or which at certain periods of history may have been attached, to certain terms. Or it may have become necessary to apply established words to new ideas, as was the case with many Greek words when used by Paul, or other early Christians; or as is the case with the word travelling since the invention of steam cars. Some commentators say travelling includes travelling by land or water, on foot, on any animal, or drawn or supported by any animal. The word travelling, therefore, if used in a law, for instance, in a penal law, which provides peculiar protection for travellers, may require interpretation, since the introduction of travelling by steam. The counsel of a prisoner charged with a crime on the highway might argue, that severer penalties are inflicted for crimes of this class only on account of the traveller's distance from people who might assist him, as would be the case in a populous place, but that on railroads, a large number of people always travel together, and hence the law need not afford additional protection, which in this case being greater severity, ought not to be furnished. Indeed, it might be of very great importance, and yet not so easy to determine, because the life of an individual may depend upon it, whether railroads are highways in the meaning of the penal law.

There are many words used by some religious sects or communities in America, in a manner, in which they are not common with the community at large. Other words again have not acquired with the people themselves a perfectly definite meaning. Not long ago, an individual in New-England left a legacy for the benefit of the poor of his place, but only to those poor who are of 'the household of faith.' See John Pickering's Lecture on the alleged Uncertainty of the Law, Boston, 1834. This expression has either not acquired a very definite meaning with the people, who use it; or if it have, those who do not use it by way of sectarian terminology, are unable to connect an idea with it, so clear as to allow of legal action.

VIII. We may not be fully acquainted with the language in which something is written, with the precise bearing or shade of meaning which certain words have in a foreign idiom or had in that language, at a particular period, or with a particular author.

The person who speaks or writes, may not be decidedly clear himself on what he speaks or writes; he may not be fully master of the subject. His ideas, therefore, may yet be vacillating, so that the different parts of what he utters, are not strictly consistent with one another.

It may be the intention of the speaker or writer, not to speak plainly, from kindness, fear, cunning, malice, caution, as in times of war or revolution, or any other motive. He may be desirous of leaving to him, whom he addresses, a choice of means or actions; or he may purposely express himself vaguely, so that at some future period, he may be at liberty to resort to one or the other meaning, according to convenience or interest.

IX. Decorum, especially, may be the reason of not expressing ourselves so plainly and distinctly, as a knowledge of the subject and mastery of the language would otherwise enable us to do.

Thus the Prussian Code, Vol. ii. Tit. xx. 1069, says:

———' And other unnatural sins of a similar kind, which cannot be mentioned here, on account of their vileness, demand an utter extinction of their memory.'[1]

Pope Innocent III, writing against the abominable and indecent swearing in France in the thirteenth century, and threatening his displeasure, says in his letter: 'they utter things in their oaths which we cannot mention.'[2]

X. It may be the object of the utterer, to clothe the true sense in various tropes, in metaphors, allegories, as poets frequently do. Or it may not be possible to express, what we wish to say, in any better way, than by an approximation to it, by way of tropes or other figurative language.

The speaker or writer may, purposely or involuntarily, use such words as would express far more than his calm and settled opinion, were they to be taken literally, or were not great deduction to be made from them.

We may be but imperfectly or not at all acquainted with the subject, to which the words of the discourse relate, for instance to customs, persons or events of nations, removed from us at a great distance either by space or time.

(1) That the reader may not misunderstand the expression 'utter extinction,' I will add that the criminal besides his other punishment, is banished for ever from the place of his former residence, where his crime has become known.

(2) Innocentii III. Epistolæ, Balusii edit. Tom. II. p. 735.

The speaker or writer may not have the opportunity of acquiring a perfect knowledge of the subject, he treats of, as was the case with many ancient grants.

If a text is obscure from the loss or interpolation of certain passages, it is not by interpretation that we can remedy the evil, as will appear from the definition which has been given.

XI. It appears, then, from the foregoing remarks, that obscurity of sense may arise, either from a want of knowledge of the subject (either in the speaker or hearer, the writer or reader,) or from an imperfect knowledge of the means of communication, (again, either in the speaker or writer, on the one hand, or the hearer or reader on the other.) And farther, that interpretation of some sort or other is always requisite, whenever human language is used; because no absolute language, by which is meant 'that mode of expression, which absolutely says all and every thing to be said, and absolutely excludes every thing else, is possible, except in one branch of human knowledge, namely, mathematics. Owing to the peculiar character of this science, its terms express the precise idea to be expressed, neither more nor less. Its language is always sufficient for the subject it treats of, because it proceeds in inventing, and has to do with the understanding alone, but not with the subjects of real life, nor with the feelings, the nobler reasoning powers, the many interests and' motives of man, the lowness or the elevation of the human soul, and their thousand intricate ramifications.

If it is certain that interpretation of some sort or other cannot be dispensed with, wherever human language is used, except in mathematics, the necessary consequence will be, that we have to ascertain the principles of true and safe interpretation. Important as it is in all spheres of human activity or knowledge, it is peculiarly so where written rules of action are given, as in religious, moral, or political codes, laws, wills, contracts, and treaties, or when works or documents of distant tribes or by-gone ages lie before us, in history and philology.

XII. It has not escaped the observation of the lawgivers of different nations, that owing to the different interpretation, put upon the same laws, much vexation and trouble arise. In fact, the ' uncertainty of the law,' which originates in a great measure from the different interpretation to which one and the same law may be subject, has become proverbial. It has been, therefore, the anxious desire of several well-disposed legislators, to avoid interpretation and consequent commentaries, by framing codes of law which should be so complete and exact as to render interpretation superfluous. To diminish litigation, and to make lawyers comparatively useless, was one of the objects of the Prussian code, promulgated by Frederick the Great. Napoleon said, according to the Mémorial de St. Hélene, by Las Cases, that he once entertained the idea, that all principles of law might be reduced to a few concise forms, which ought to be combined according to fixed rules, similar to those of mathematics; and that thus simplicity and certainty of law might be established. He soon, however, gave up the idea, when he came to discuss the various parts of the French civil code, with the other members of the committee appointed to draw up that work. In Bavaria, commentaries on the penal code are actually prohibited. With true wisdom did the government of that country officially publish the motives, explanations, &c., which were given in the course of the discussions in the king's privy council, for adopting the various laws. They have been drawn up and reduced to a systematic whole, published in three volumes, Munich, 1813, and 1814. But it was not equally wise to prohibit commentaries; for those who advised the king so to do, forgot, that as they felt bound to explain the various provisions of the code, so would their own explanations again carry along with them the necessity of interpretation, simply because drawn up in human language, though we willingly allow, not in the same degree with the briefer code. No code can possibly provide for all specific cases, which most frequently consist of a combination of simple elements; nearly every case in reality is a complex one; and because the various relations of men are forever changing.

This remarkable prohibition of commentaries in Bavaria, is to be found in the royal mandate of October 19, 1813, by Maximilian Joseph, to all the courts of appeal, printed before the Notes to the Penal Code for the kingdom of Bavaria, according to the Protocols of the royal Privy Council, 3 vols. Munich, 1813, 1814. It reads thus:

'We, therefore, direct you, with regard to all points which depend upon the interpretation of the penal code, the sense and motive of a legal distinction, and the principles of their application, to refer to the notes, and expressly to mention the respective passage of the notes should you have to make any report for inquiry as to a doubtful point. And it is our express order, that besides this exposition, ordered by ourselves, no officer of the state, or private scholar, shall publish a commentary on the penal code, and that the courts, in trying and judging penal cases, as well as the professors of our Universities in their lectures, shall rely exclusively on the text of the code with reference to the notes, so that the penal code be applied and taught in the same spirit in all parts of our kingdom, and according to that which we have been pleased to ordain and explain.' Still the royal mandate continues immediately thus:—

'We charge you carefully to collect that which, in occurring cases, may appear to you especially important or doubtful, and to send the same, at the conclusion of the first year directly to us, with remarks upon it.'

In a similar spirit, and with equally good intention, it was formerly not considered advisable, in Prussia, to allow professors of law to lecture in the Universities on the code, for fear that scientific comments should lead to perplexity, and thus defeat one of the main objects of the code—simplicity of law. Mr. de Savigny was, I believe, the first Prussian jurist, who delivered lectures on the code of Frederic; he began them about the year 1819, if I recollect right.

XIII. It would, indeed, be a subject greatly to be deplored if it were possible—happily it is not—

to produce a code so constructed as to be closed for ever. It is one of the most efficient agents in the civil progress of a nation, that, certain principles being established, they should be left to unfold themselves gradually, and to be expanded, modified, and limited, by the civil action of the nation itself, by the practical political intercourse of society. On this subject more will be said hereafter; in the present place I beg only to add, in order not to be misunderstood, that I am as zealous an advocate of the certainty of law as any citizen can be, who loves clear right, and, therefore, is anxious to know it. For this reason, in part, I am endeavoring to establish principles of interpretation, or to make them known in a wider circle. I hold myself fully convinced of the great benefit, which a wise code may bestow upon a nation, if made at the proper period of maturity of a nation for that purpose; if it contain the essence, the settlement, perfection, improvement, and expansion, of the law, already existing in some shape, way, or form, and be not a futile invention of the closet; and if the law-makers do not believe thereby to forestall all future expansion of the law. A code is not a herbarium, in which we deposit law like dried plants. Let a code be the fruit grown out of the civil life of a nation, and containing the seed for future growth.

CHAPTER II.—SECTION XIV. 45

The impossibility of closing the law, as it were, has already been acknowledged. In France, and in Prussia many large volumes of complements (*Ergänzungen*) have been officially published, and are annually adding to the code.

Never has interpretation been dispensed with; never can it be dispensed with. This necessity lies in the nature of things, of our mind and our language; and in those countries where codes have been established, as in France, Bavaria, Austria, Prussia, &c., some authority is always designated from which, in doubtful cases, explanations shall be obtained; as the council of state, the minister of justice, or some law committee appointed for that purpose.

XIV. The Austrian civil code, introduction, paragraph 8, says, 'The lawgiver alone has the authority of giving an interpretation of general and binding authority. An interpretation of this sort is to be applied to all cases yet to be decided, if the lawgiver does not add expressly, that his interpretation shall not apply to the decision of those cases which treat of actions done, or rights claimed, before the interpretation took place.'

The Prussian code says, introduction, paragraph 47, 'If the judge finds the proper sense of the law ambiguous, he has to inform the law committee of his doubts, and to ask for its decision, without, however, mentioning the litigating parties.' Paragraph 48, 'The judge of inquiry is bound to found his decision in the case upon the judgment of the law committee; the parties, however, retain their right of resorting to the usual remedies.'

Several of these provisions have been adopted from the Roman law. The Roman Emperor decided doubtful cases, which had been reported to him in writing, by '*decreta.*' See Li. 1. *ff de Const. Princ.* L. *fin. pr. de Legib.* See, also, 1 Blackstone, 59.

The civilians say, 'Est autem non raro necessaria legis interpretatio; quam solus quidem facit legislator, in quantum interpretatio vim legis habitura est. Quo respicit, quod scriptum est, uti leges condere, ita et easdem interpretari, solo imperio dignum esse.' Voet Comment. ad Pandectas, Li. Tit. III. 18, and every other commentator of the *Corpus Juris*.

The late Mr. Edward Livingston provides in his penal code that 'if any penal law shall be so inaccurately drawn, as to bring within its penalty an act that it would not, in the opinion of the court, have been the intention of the legislature, so to punish, the accused must be acquitted; but the court shall report such case to the legislature at their next session, or within eight days, if they be in session.' Code of crimes and punishments, Book I. chap. 1, art. 9, or page 367 of his system of penal law for the State of Louisiana, Philadelphia, 1833. See, also, his introductory report to the code of crimes and punishments, ibid. p. 139. As to interpretation in general, it seems evident that Mr. Livingston relied too much on the possible perspicuity of human speech. He, as well as Mr. Jeremy Bentham, appears not to have a perfectly correct idea of human language, and its exact relation to things and thoughts. They seem to have imagined that the same degree of clearness of speech, which we find in mathematics, might be obtained in all branches, forgetting, perhaps, in how limited a circle mathematics move, or they would lose at once the character of absolute distinctness. Having said thus much, we cannot leave this topic, without guarding ourselves against a misapprehension that we undervalue the merits of these two reflecting men. No lawyer, or politician ought to remain unacquainted with their works, for, whatever reason he may find to dissent from them, in many particulars, he will find enough worthy of being gathered and stored up. We have frequently found that their works are treated with a degree of superciliousness, which can be explained only by a want of acquaintance with them.

XV. If these various authorities have the power of interpretation, and if this interpretation has effect not only for the future, but also upon the case, respecting which the doubt arises, as is the case with the several nations above mentioned, then the English and Americans consider this manner of interpreting contrary to their constitutional spirit. It approaches, in their opinion, too much to the dangerous union of the attributes of the legislator and the judge; though, strange to say, this very fear, so just and salutary in its kind, has, in some cases, led precisely to the end that was to be avoided. For the many constructive offences, for example, in the old English law, were little less than the product of legislating judges. The independence of the judiciary is one of the touchstones of civil liberty; but in these cases, the judges did not only act as independent judges dependent upon the law, but they left their proper province, and trespassed upon that of the lawgiver.[1]

Those who imagine that the uncertainty of law can possibly be avoided, by avoiding all ambiguity of language, forget that, as it was said already, most cases present a compound of simple cases, and furthermore, that the uncertainty of law arises not

---

(1) On the Independence of the Judiciary, and the Progress of Law, see Political Ethics, vol. I. the proper chapters.

only out of the general uncertainty of human speech, but frequently also out of the ambiguous terminology of other sciences, arts, &c. Should the law settle before-hand the meaning of all terms? And what is to be done with reference to the new things and relations, which are discovered, invented, or established, and must, in suits which may occur, be classed under some head or other acknowledged by the law? If in an important insurance case the question has arisen, whether the Bermudas belong to the West Indies or not, and, upon inquiry, it was found that the geographical books differed on this point, was the ambiguity in this case the fault of the law, or could it possibly have been avoided by the wisest foresight of the most profound lawgiver, or the most comprehensive plan of a code? The law could only then be absolutely certain, when mankind had ceased to be a living, moving society—a society, whose very existence depends upon an infinite entwining and interweaving of countless interests.

XVI. At all times there have existed many people who, seeing how often in matters of law, as in all other branches, the formality is seized upon instead of the spirit, or being desirous of flattering unguarded crowds, declaim against the niceties of the law, and with it against careful interpretation, as being mere subtleties of the lawyers to harass litigating parties and draw their own profit from a protracted administration of justice. No one who knows the least of the history of judicial administration, or has had an opportunity to observe it in some countries at the present time, will venture to deny, that no branch of government has been at some periods and is to this day in some countries—witness for instance Spain and the Spanish colonies, or Germany at the time of the Peasants War, or England when the Star Chamber flourished most, for instance under Charles I.—more scandalously diverted from its real course, has been a greater evil to the community, for the weal of which alone it is established, than the judiciary department. Lawyers have at times formed an almost invincible legion of harpies. But in viewing evils and endeavoring to find remedies, we must carefully avoid the creating of equally great or greater ones. Again and again have the people been told to throw off their fetters, and to have justice done by plain men of common sense, and unsophisticated minds. From ancient times down to the latest, to our own period, it has been asserted, that if the real question were to award true justice according to the simple merits of the case, and not to satisfy technicalities, the difficulty would not be great and lawyers might probably be dispensed with. These persons desire, in fact, a patriarchal administration of justice—the worst of all justice beyond the family circle and in a society at all advanced in civilization. If we examine their desire more closely we shall find that nothing less is demanded than constructive justice, constructive laws, constructive verdicts and constructive penalties, or which is equally bad, the substitution of individual feelings and views for the general rule and even law. Nay, they substantially desire ex post facto justice declared permanent. The declamations against law and lawyers rest essentially upon the same erroneous principle, upon which absolute monarchists found their claims and desires. They wish for a paternal government, a monarch who may rule, untrammelled by fundamental laws, according to the fatherly desire of his heart. Let the king be unfettered to do good, let nothing bind him but his conscience; let him be responsible to no one but his God. All very fine—it is the Chinese rule—parental care, filial obedience—only, do not talk any longer of right, of justice.

It is so frequently forgotten that there are two parties in questions of justice, and what seems so uncommonly plain to the one, that no possible doubt can exist according to his opinion, does by no means present itself in the same light to the other. Some acts are lawful in the day time, but not so during night; or they are less punishable if done during the day, than otherwise. If the law at the same time says that night shall be from sunset to sunrise, it seems to be as plain as human language can be. Yet there were not long ago two parties contending in an Irish court, the one maintaining that sunrise means, with regard to the place in question, the rising of the sun above the neighboring mountains, while the other partly insisted that sunrise means the time which is indicated as such in the almanac. Both parties probably thought that nothing could be plainer than the respective view which each took, for the very reason that it was of great importance to each to carry his view. In England, it has been settled by act of parliament, in 1837, that night, with regard to burglary, comprehends the space of time from nine in the evening till six in the morning, all the year round. But what is nine o'clock? A life may depend upon showing that a certain act was done at half past eight and nine o'clock.

The freer a country, the more necessary becomes interpretation. For one of the main ingredients of civil liberty, and at the same time one of its greatest blessings, is the protection against individual passion, violence, views, opinions, caprice or well meant but disturbing interference—the supremacy of law.

This, however, involves the condition that laws once made, must be administered by others than those who made them, or are making new ones. Without it, the law ceases to be a guarantee; but if the making and administering are separate, it is necessary that the laws be interpreted, and to do this justly and conscientiously, the ministers of the law must proceed by proper, safe and sound rules.[1] In those states where the law making power is the same with the law administering, interpretation in the highest spheres of judicial action is comparatively unimportant; for the will of the supreme power may at any time be substituted for the law, or may decide any doubtful case according to whatever seems expedient to it.

(1) Connected with this fact is the other, which I have touched upon in vol. i. of the Polit. Ethics, that no country has risen in political civilization without the institution of the advocate. Indeed, its very existence proves a considerable step in civilization, because it shows not only that the judge being versed in the law, an equal chance shall be given to the litigating or accused party; in my opinion, it indicates something more; it manifests a degree of acknowledgment that the law shall be the immutable rule—a rule above the judge, not one within his breast. When the European race rose out of the confusion of feudal independence, and law became gradually acknowledged as the supreme rule, and yet the subject not being properly understood, and when, as the same dialectic subtlety which had stolen into all branches, into philosophy as well as theology, the general bent of the European mind very naturally manifested itself likewise in the department of the law. Lawyers actually became, in many instances, the perverters of right, instead of being its protectors. Satire was directed on all sides against them. Not a witty poet who did not discharge his arrows against them, not a carnival in which they were not ridiculed, and not unjustly so. But let us not forget that precisely the

same amount of satire, at the same period, was directed in the same vehicles against matrimony. Does any one of us, nevertheless, doubt the necessity of marriage as the very first element of civilization? Lawyers have at times pressed upon society like a very night mare. They and the ministers of the church have been the worst counsellors of tyranny, the worst flatterers of absolutism, but let us weigh tne matter well, and I believe we shall come to the conclusion that the cause of liberty owes to lawyers likewise infinite gratitude. Certainly it is a fact, that if English tyranny, in whatever character it showed itself, has been supported by lawyers, the cause of British liberty has been rescued in a great measure by them.

CHAPTER III.

Construction.—Its Definition.—Twofold Application of this Definition.—Necessity of Construction, when Interpretation ceases to avail.—Necessity of distinguishing between Interpretation and Construction.—Instance.—Doctrine of Cy-pres. Science of Hermeneutics.—Derivation of the word.—Construction, although dangerous, yet indispensable.—Different Species of Interpretation, to arrive at the True Sense.—Close Interpretation.—Literal Interpretation is an inadmissible Term.—Instances of pretended Literal Interpretation.—Extensive Interpretation.—Liberal Interpretation not a good Term.—Extravagant Interpretation.—Limited and Free Interpretation.—Predestined Interpretation.—Artful Interpretation.—Authentic Interpretation.—Different Species of Theologic Interpretation.—Close, Comprehensive, Transcendant, Extravagant Construction.—Indemnity Bills.

I. The definition, which has been given of the term interpretation, shows that it can only take place, if the text conveys some meaning or other. It happens, however, not unfrequently, that in comparing two different writings of the same individual, or body of men, they are found to contain contradictions, and yet are not intended to contradict one another. Or it happens that a part of a writing or declaration contradicts the rest, for instance, some provisions of laws issued even by so high a body as the British parliament. When this is the case, and the nature of the document, declaration, or whatever else it may be, is such as not to allow us to consider the whole as being invalidated by a partial or other contradiction, we must resort to construction. Construction is likewise our guide, if we are bound to act in cases which have not been foreseen, by the framers of those rules, by which we are nevertheless obliged, for some binding reason, faithfully to regulate, as well as we can, our actions respecting the unforeseen case ; for instance, when we have to act in politics bound by a constitution in a case which presents features entirely new and unforeseen.

II. Construction is the drawing of conclusions respecting subjects, that lie beyond the direct expression of the text, from elements known from and given in the text—conclusions which are in the spirit, though not within the letter of the text.

Thus we say, 'you cannot construe his refusal into a general unkind disposition towards you,' which means, you cannot draw the conclusion, that the utterer is unfavorably disposed to you (the subject which lies beyond the direct expression of the text) from the specific refusal in the present case (the elements known and given in the text.)

In politics, construction signifies generally the supplying of supposed or real imperfections, or insufficiencies of a text, according to proper principles and rules. By insufficiency, we understand, both imperfect provision for the cases, which might or ought to have been provided for, and the inadequateness of the text for cases which human wisdom could not foresee, as for instance, the application of a very ancient charter to cases arising out of entirely and radically new relations, which have since sprung up, and which cases, nevertheless, clearly belong to that province of human actions for which the charter was intended.

If we apply the above definition of construction to texts of inferior authority or importance, which partially militate with the demands of superior authority, we shall see, that construction is the causing of the text to agree and harmonize with the demands or principles of superior authority, although they are not, according to the immediate and direct meaning of the words constituting the text, contained in it.

It is, as will be seen presently, construction alone which saves us, in many instances, from sacrificing the spirit of a text or the object, to the letter of the text, or the means by which that object was to be obtained, and without construction, written laws, in fact any laws or other texts, containing rules of actions, specific or general, would, in many cases, become fearfully destructive to the best and wisest intentions, nay, frequently, produce the very opposite of what it was purposed to effect.

III. The definition which has been given, involves the fact that the constructor is not allowed to proceed without rule or arbitrarily; he has to draw conclusions (of course correct and faithful ones) from the elements given in the text. This, if properly analyzed or applied, gives us all the necessary rules of true construction.

The proper principles of construction are those which ought to guide us in good faith and conscience. They may be twofold, according to what has been seen in section ii :

1. If the text is itself a declaration of the fundamental principles, which we are bound to follow in a certain sphere of actions, and of certain fundamental forms, which are to regulate our actions, in this case, construction signifies the discovery of the spirit, principles, and rules, that ought to guide us according to the text, with regard to subjects, on which that declaration is silent, but which neverthe-

CHAPTER III.—SECTION III. 59

less belongs to its province. If, for instance, a political constitution or charter has been adopted or granted, to regulate our political actions, and a case occurs, which has not been directly provided for, but which is of an undoubted political character, we have faithfully to search for its true spirit, and act accordingly in the case under consideration. Analogy, or rather parallel reasoning[1] in this signification of construction, is the essential means of effecting it.

2. Or there may exist principles or rules of superior authority, and the problem of construction then is to cause that which is to be construed to agree with them. In this case the principles and rules of superior authority are the 'subjects that lie beyond the direct expression of the text' mentioned in the definition.

For instance, morality is one of the chief ends of all human life; without it no state can exist. This is the superior principle. If, therefore, a testator leaves a will, containing provisions of an immoral

---

(1) It will be observed that analogy in this case signifies something very different from that reasoning by analogy, against which the author declared himself strongly in his Pol. Ethics. There he spoke against reasoning on comparisons of totally different things; here he speaks of subjects belonging to the same sphere. Indeed, analogy in the present case means nothing more than a reasoning by proportion. In the case, provided for by law, or decided already, we have: If A and B exist, then D shall take place. In the case to be construed we have E, similar to A, and F similar to B, hence let G be similar to D, in the same proportion.

character, striking out these provisions is called construing it, i. e. making it harmonize with the general and great object of all government, without thereby invalidating the whole will. Or if a law be passed, parts of which are contrary to the fundamental law of the state, it is called construing the law, when the proper judges declare these parts to be invalid. This is acknowledged in the United States, and in a similar manner does the civil law declare that:

'The judge shall be guided by the strictness of the law, and not consider what the emperor has declared against the law.'—C. III. Tit. 1, *de jud.* 11. Or

'Quae facta laedunt pietatem, existimationem, verecundiam nostram et (ut generaliter dixerim) contra bonos mores fiunt, nec facere nos posse credendum est.'—[Papineau's Digest, L. xxviii. t. 7, 15.

If the codes of some countries declare, that if in certain cases the judge can find no law precisely applicable, he shall be guided by the spirit of the provisions enacted for those cases, which resemble most that under consideration, they authorize construction according to the first part of our first definition. The Austrian code prescribes the mode just mentioned. See the same Introduction, 7. In penal judicature no legal action can take place in a case unprovided for by law; yet the Chinese code applies construction of this sort even to offences and crimes. See Sir George T. Staunton's Penal Code of China, sect. XLIV. p. 43.

Also treaties are sometimes made, defining the boundaries of countries imperfectly known, which, when they come to be acted upon; are found to contain language not applicable to the actual state of things, in which case we must have recourse to construction.

IV. In the most general adaptation of the term, construction signifies the representing of an entire whole from given elements by just conclusions. Thus it is said, ' a few actions may sometimes suffice to construe the whole character of a man.'

It was not without repeatedly weighing the subject, that I first ventured upon the distinction between interpretation and construction ; for, if clear distinction is one of the efficient means to arrive at truth, it is equally true that subtleties impede instead of aiding in seizing upon it. Many political contests, however, in which both parties seemed to me equally honest, as well as frequent disputes in law, led me to the distinction, and I had the great satisfaction of finding that since the first publication of the present tract, two of our most distinguished lawyers have fully concurred in the distinction between the two, and have adopted it.

It appears that many law cases would be settled with greater ease, and to the greater satisfaction of the interested parties, if this distinction were strictly kept in view. We have first to settle whether construction is at all admissible, or whether it be absolutely indispensable, as, I believe it has been seen, in many cases, it actually is. After this we have to settle whether in the given case, interpretation suffices, or whether we must have recourse to construction. The following case is in point:

A gentleman whom we may call Thomas Cumming, a bachelor, and a native of Great Britain, accumulated a considerable fortune in the United States; he died, and his testament showed that he had bequeathed a large sum to 'his nephew, Thomas Cumming,' in England. The latter was dead at the time of the making of his uncle's will in America, leaving, however, an only child, likewise called Thomas Cumming; but the death of the one and the birth of the other were equally unknown to Thomas Cumming, the eldest, at the time when he made his testament, and down to the time of his decease. Now it was contended that T. Cumming, the testator, did not leave the sum to T. Cumming, the nephew, he being already dead; and that the birth of the youngest

Cumming, not yet being known to the testator, he could not have meant him. It is evident that according to the true import of the term interpretation, the argument was good; for according to the true meaning of the testator's words, that is according to the meaning which he attached to them, he cannot have meant T. Cumming the youngest. But there being no T. Cumming, whom the testator meant, in existence, the question becomes, how shall we draw our conclusions and apply them to the subject, which lies beyond the direct expression of the text, from elements known by and given in the text,—the testament in the present case? Is the testament our guide or not? It evidently is; then construction becomes necessary if interpretation is insufficient, and the elements afforded us by the text will lead us to the just and true conclusion, that Thomas Cumming the eldest, meant to leave the respective sum to the English branch of his family, and that T. Cumming the youngest, ought to receive it.

The whole doctrine of Cy-pres belongs to construction. See Story on Equity, 2, 415.

Nor does the distinction do violence to language, whether we view the two terms as used in common life, or respecting their etymology; for construction, from *construere*, means to build up, from *con* and *struo*. Lawyers frequently call both construction;

divines, on the other hand, use interpretation for both.

V. That branch of science which establishes the principles and rules of interpretation and constructruction, is called *hermeneutics*, from the Greek ἑρμηνευω to explain, to interpret ; and the actual application of them *exegesis*, from the Greek ἐξήγησις explanation. Hermeneutics and exegesis stand in the relation to each other as theory and practice.

In England and America these terms are generally used by theologians only, but the Germans, who first brought them into use, apply them equally to philology and divinity. There is no reason why this term should not be used in all sciences, in which interpretation and construction become necessary, in short in all branches in which we are bound carefully to ascertain the sense of words, and regulate actions according to their spirit and true import.

VI. For the very reason that construction endeavors to arrive at conclusions beyond the absolute sense of the text, and that it is dangerous on this account, we must strive the more anxiously to find out safe rules, to guide us on the dangerous path. For, although dangerous, we cannot possibly escape it, because times, relations, things change, and cannot be foreseen by human intellect, nor is it given to any man to provide for all cases already existing, or use such language which shall leave no doubt. Many things are dangerous, yet we cannot dispense with them nevertheless.

It lies likewise in the nature of things, that in many cases, interpretation and construction must closely approach to one another, still the distinction is clear. Food and poison are very distinct things, although in some cases they approach so closely, that it would be difficult to decide with absolute certainty, which term we ought to choose.

That from the nature of interpretation and construction, since they signify the arriving at something certain from something ambiguous or uncertain, good faith and common sense are indispensable in the application of the principles furnished by hermeneutics, to the complex cases of practical life, is evident. More on this subject will be presently given.

VII. An individual may use some words, which every one understands, and which for the case are sufficiently clear; but if you were to ask him as to the exact limits to which he wishes to see his remarks extended, or to put to him a number of cases in progressive connexion with each other, he himself will be doubtful in most instances, how far he would extend the application of his remark. The conse quence is, that interpretation may be according to the more or less comprehensive sense, which we give to the words of various kinds, not, be it mentioned here in anticipation, that the object of interpretation can ever vary, or that there can be two true meanings in any text. The sole legitimate object of all interpretation is to find out the true sense and meaning, not to impart them; but since this true sense is occult, we may be bound to use various means to arrive at it to the best of our ability, and according to the conscientious desire of finding the true sense. Accordingly, we have to note the following different species of interpretation.

VIII. Close Interpretation (interpretatio restrictiva,) if just reasons, connected with the formation and character of the text, induce us to take the words in their narrowest meaning.

This species of interpretation has been generally called literal interpretation, a term inadmissible, in my opinion. Literal interpretation ought to mean of course, that which takes the words in their literal sense, which is hardly ever possible, since all human language is made up of tropes, allusions, images, expressions relating to erroneous conceptions, &c., for instance, the sun rises. Literal interpretation would signify, moreover, in most cases, a contradition, since there can be but little doubt as to the meaning of a sentence, if the words are to be taken in a literal signification, and thus make sense at all. Interpretation, therefore, would be superfluous. On the other hand, it is very difficult to say where the literal signification of a word ends, and the figurative begins. In reading Latin no one would insist that the literal sense of Confutare is to check boiling water by pouring in cold from a vessel called *futum*, or *futis*, although this was the original signification. In other cases, it would be difficult to say what is the literal meaning. Is the word *going*, if used of a vessel proceeding from one place to another, used in its literal sense or not? If we substitute original meaning for literal, we find at once the impropriety of the term. To Give is a word found in all Teutonic and many other languages, and is, probably, derived from the ancient word Gaff, the hollow of the hand, so that the original meaning is identical with our word to Hand. But is, on this account, the expression 'I give,' used in a will, to be declared void, although sound reasons may prevail to adopt the closest possible interpretation, because the testator, being dead, cannot any longer *give*, in its literal sense, something to another person, because he cannot use any longer his hands? Or are we to make a distinction between original and literal meaning? If so, where are the limits, and what possible good can we derive from it?

These remarks are not without practical importance. Enormous crimes, and egregious follies have been committed under the pretended sanction of literal interpretation, using interpretation as a means to promote certain objects, while its simple and only object is to ascertain and fix the true sense of a text.

When that poor tavern keeper in England, whose inn had the sign of a crown, was sentenced for treason, because he had jestingly said, that he had made his son heir to the crown, his judges thought they interpreted literally, and maintained that it was a case which called for literal interpretation. Had they used the term close interpretation, they could never have reached the life of the poor tavern keeper, at least in this way. For the closer the interpretation was taken, the closer it would have come to his tavern crown. Literal interpretation is a most deceptive term; under the guise of strict adherence to the words, it wrenches them from their sense.

If we understand by literal interpretation, a species, which by way of adhering to the letter, substitutes a false sense for the true one, it has no more meaning than the term 'false facts.' It is false, deceptive, or artful interpretation, if we do not give that sense to words which they ought to have, according to good faith, common sense, the use which the utterer made of them, &c.

The canon law prohibits the ministers of the Roman Catholic church from shedding human blood. Many bishops and other ecclesiastics of the middle ages, therefore, who could not resist the universal spirit of warfare and robbery of those times, for instance, of the 11th and 12th centuries, fought with maces, without thorns or points. Philippe-de-Dreux, bishop of Beauvais, for instance, a redoubted warrior, and famous for his robberies and cruelties, killed in the battle of Bouvines, every one he could reach with his mace. Wulson, author of the Heroic Science, speaks of this usage as generally received.[1]

---

(1) See, among other works, Histoire Civile, Physique et Morale de Paris, by T. A. Dulaure, Paris, 1825, 3d ed. vol. ii. p. 415 et seq.

According to a similar misinterpretation, as it seems to me, the same law was held to prohibit priests from practising surgery, but not medicine, as they frequently did in earlier times, when priests were the few who possessed any science whatever. If there was no particular reason for this distinction, which I do not know, the fault arose out of the omission of paying attention to the *usus loquendi*. Single words were taken in their respective significations, but it was not literal interpretation for all that. Shedding blood is not the opening of veins or arteries, but the doing it with violence to the harm of the wounded.

Innumerable dogmatic aberrations from the path of religion, have had and have their origin in this species of misinterpretation. The above instance brings another to my mind, likewise belonging to the history of the catholic church, though quite as many instances may be found in law, if we refer to the time of the schoolmen.

IX. Extensive interpretation (interpretatio extensiva,) called likewise liberal interpretation, when it inclines towards adopting the more or most comprehensive signification of the word. Extensive or comprehensive interpretation seems to be a better term than liberal interpretation. The latter sounds as if a disposition of the interpreter were to be indicated, while his true object is to ascertain the exact meaning; at least the term ought to be reserved for those cases where we actually strive, for some reason or other, to give the most liberal sense to a set of words, for instance in a case which strongly calls for mercy, though the law is distinct and demands punishment.

Extravagant interpretation (interpretatio excedens)

> It was one of the monastic punishments to wall up the criminal alive. This was called '*In pace,*' at least with the Franciscans, because every member said: In pace requiescat, when the fearful ceremony was concluded, and the last brick immured the criminal, never to return. It has not frequently occurred, but sometimes it actually has. The annals of the Franciscans say that even their saint threatened a brother, who refused to visit a leprous man, with this punishment. The reason why the order preferred this punishment was because: Ecclesia non sitit sanguinem (the church thirsteth not for blood); they preferred, therefore, this, in appearance, less violent infliction of death. But even if the actual infliction of death were less violent than hanging—although most persons will believe that immuring must greatly protract the last agony of death, and give full time to the horrors of despair—the interpretation of *sitire sanguinem* would not be more correct, simply because Sanguis stands here as part for the whole, namely, Death. Ordres monastiques, vol. iii.

CHAPTER III.—SECTION IX. 71

is that mode of interpreting, which substitutes such meaning as is evidently beyond the true meaning; it is, therefore, not genuine interpretation.

Interpretation may, likewise, be limited or free.

Free or unrestricted (interpretation soluta) proceeds simply on the general principles of interpretation in good faith, not bound by any specific or superior principle. Limited or restricted interpretation (interpretatio limitata) takes place, if other rules or principles than the strictly hermeneutic ones, limit us.

If, for instance, an individual were to say, ' I neither believe nor disbelieve the bible, but intend to find out its true sense, and then to be determined whether I shall believe in it or not,' it would be unrestricted interpretation. If, however, the inquirer has already come to the conclusion, that the scriptures were written by inspired men, that, therefore, no real contradiction can exist in the bible, and he interprets certain passages accordingly, which *prima facie* may appear to involve a contradiction, it would be limited interpretation. See Ernesti, Institutio Interpretis, part i. section i. chap. ix.

All proclamations, orders, &c. of a British monarch or the government of the United States, are subject to interpretation restricted or limited by the acts of parliament or congress, if they require interpretation at all, and would otherwise clash with these acts.

X. Finally, interpretation may be predestined (interpretatio predestinata,) if the interpreter, either consciously or unknown to himself, yet laboring under a strong bias of mind, makes the text subservient to his preconceived views, or some object he desires to arrive at. Luther, in his work, De Papatu, charges the catholics with what is called here, predestined interpretation, of the bible, inasmuch as in his view, they do not seek for the true meaning of the bible, but strive to make it subservient to their preconceived dogmas. This peculiar species of interpretation would not have been mentioned here, for it is not genuine interpretation, were it not so common in all branches, in sciences and common life, in law and politics not less than in religion, with protestants as habitually as with catholics, so that none of us can be too watchful against being betrayed into it. It corresponds to what might be called in ratiocination, ex post facto reasoning.

A peculiar species of predestined interpretation is artful interpretation (interpretatio vafer,) that, which, by cunning and art, attempts to show that the text means something, which was not according to the interpreter's own knowledge the meaning of the author or utterer. Artful interpretation is not always immoral. A legal counsel is understood to produce everything favorable that can be brought to bear upon the case of his client, so that, the same being done on the other side, all that can be said for and against the subject, may be brought before the judges. That counsel ought not to swerve from the common principles of morality in this, as in any other case, is evident. We shall give in this work our views of the duties of legal counsel.

The same remark does not apply to political party affairs, for this simple reason, that in matters of law final judgment is given by, and the arguments on both sides are stated before, the same judges at the same time, and before judges who form no party themselves, or belong to none of the contending parties. The comparing of political party-matters either to legal strifes or to real warfare is unsound in principle, and has created great mischief. It must be counted among the many subjects, which have done infinite injury to society by a confusion of ideas and words, and a misapplication of similes in their departments. If we see violent party struggles, and the advocates on both sides maintaining the authority of the same instrument, perhaps of the same provision, let us ask ourselves, which of the two proceeds on genuine and which on artful interpretation, which proceeds upon the instrument itself, and which has some distant object beyond it, or starts from some preconceived views or interested motives. Frequently this inquiry alone will contribute essentially to our arriving at the real state of things.

XI. Authentic interpretation is called that which proceeds from the author or utterer of the text himself; properly speaking, therefore, it is no interpretation, but a declaration. If a legislative body, or monarch, give an interpretation, it is called authentic, though the same individuals who issued the law to be interpreted, may not give the interpretation; because the successive assemblies or monarchs are considered as one and the same, making the law and giving the interpretation in their representative, and not in their personal characters. Authentic interpretation, therefore, need not always be correct, though it has, if formally given, binding power. Still it may be reversed by a subsequent law.

According to the means which we make use of to assist us in interpretation, we find with some writers the following species: *interpretatio usualis*, if we interpret on the ground of usage, *doctrinalis*, if in a scientific way, *grammatica, historica, historico-grammatica, logica. Interpretatio declarativa* is that interpretation which settles the meaning of a term. until then of vague or ambiguous signification,

e. g. the word *game* having been used, it is finally settled what animals shall be classed under this head, and which not.

Some authors, for instance, Rutherforth, have divided interpretation into three kinds, literal, rational, and mixed. These terms, however, as well as many of the above, lose greatly in their importance, or become actually inadmissible, if we adhere to our definition of interpretation, which is to find the ' true sense.' There can be then no literal sense, and besides it, another. A single word may signify indeed several things, and in order to determine in which sense it has been used in a particular passage, we shall be obliged, as a matter of course, to use grammar, etymology, logic, and every other means, which are in constant use among men, to understand the words of one another. This has been clearly shown as early as by Ernesti in his Institutes already cited. See sect. XI. I.

XII. Owing to the peculiar character which the bible possesses, as a book of history and revelation, and the relation between the old and new testaments, we find that some divines ascribe various meanings to the same passages or rites, and that different theologians take the same passage in senses of an essentially different character. We hear thus of typical, allegorical, parabolical, anagogical, moral and accommodatory senses, and of corresponding modes of interpretation. For information on this subject, the reader must refer to works on theologic hermeneutics. In politics and law we have to deal with plain words and human use of them only.

The chief subjects we have to interpret or construe, as citizens, are spoken words or entire speeches, letters, orders and directions, deeds, contracts, wills, laws, compacts and constitutions or charters, declaring and defining fundamental rights or privileges. Whether we are lawyers or not, we may be called upon to vote upon subjects requiring the interpretation of some of these; and whether we shall ever be members of legislative bodies or not, every citizen of a free country is not only permitted to form his opinion upon all prominent features of his government, fundamental laws, public men, and important measures, but it is his duty to do so. Every citizen may become an executor of a will, in which he may be called upon to interpret provisions, which materially affect the well being of large numbers of unprotected orphans, he may, in times of great importance, find himself in an office of a delicate character, and he may at any day be charged to decide upon matters of grave importance, in the most sacred character a citizen can assume, namely, as a juror. It will be found necessary, therefore, for every citizen to know how to interpret correctly and faithfully, and however brief, compared to the magnitude of the subject, this work will be, I shall nevertheless, endeavor to lay down the most essential principles, sufficient at least to direct attention to the main points.

XIII. Before we proceed to them it will be necessary to settle the meaning of some terms respecting construction. Construction is either close, comprehensive, transcendant, or extravagant, similar to the corresponding species of interpretation.

1. Close construction is that which inclines to the directest possible application of the text, or the principles it involves, to new or unprovided cases, or to contradictory parts, in short, to subjects which lie beyond the words of the text.

2. Comprehensive construction is that which inclines to an extensive application of the text, or the principles it involves, to new, unprovided, or not sufficiently specified cases or contradictions.

3. Transcendant construction is that which is derived from, or founded upon, a principle superior to the text; and, nevertheless aims at deciding on subjects belonging to the province of that text.

When, in August, 1835, the postmaster of the

city of New York applied to the postmaster general of the United States for instruction, respecting certain incendiary publications, sent by persons, usually called abolitionists, to his post office to be transmitted to the south, and retained by him (the New York postmaster,) the postmaster general answered, that there was no part of the post law, which would authorize the post establishment to decline the carriage of newspapers or other publications on account of their contents. Such interference would, in fact, amount to an interference with the 'freedom of speech, or of the press,' so distinctly guaranteed by the Constitution of the United States. See Mr. Calhoun's Report on the Attempts to circulate through the mail inflammatory Appeals, &c.; made to the Senate, February 4, 1836. Yet the postmaster general did not absolutely discountenance the measure of the New York postmaster; he only throws him on his own responsibility, arguing thus: 'The post establishment is for the convenience, intercourse, &c., of and between the people, not for their destruction; hence it ought not to aid in destructive measures.' See the letter of the postmaster general, dated August 4, 1835, to the postmasters in Charleston and in New York; among other records of the times in Niles's Weekly Register, Baltimore, August 22, 1835. The majority of the

CHAPTER III.—SECTION XIII. 79

people seem to have acquiesced in this decision, and the matter has ever since rested. It is this, that I would call transcendant construction—dangerous in the highest degree, yet at times necessary. Still, though necessary, it would be wise that each case of magnitude should be followed by an act of indemnity as it is termed in British terminology ; for, although such an act may, in many cases, be obtained by the same power of popularity, on the strength of which first the transgression of the law was ventured, it will nevertheless have its tendency to check.[1] In

---

(1) The British opposition has always, and especially in 1807, demanded that exceptions of the kind for which ministers demand afterwards acts of indemnity, must be rare, must not touch on the fundamentals of the constitution, that their necessity for the common good must be proved, and that this necessity must not be caused by ministers. In 1807, the ministers levied taxes on American imports, a month longer than allowed by the American Act. The debates on the occasion are of high interest. See Hansard Parl. Deb. vol. ix. p. 996–1001. In 1818, ministers demanded indemnity after the suspension of the habeas corpus act, not only for themselves, but for the magistrates which had acted by direction of ministers against it. Hansard, vol. xxxvii. In 1826, oats were permitted to be imported against law, on account of a failure of oats in England. For the debates on indemnity for this act against law, see Hansard, New Series, vol. xvi. In 1838, however, indemnity was thrust upon a high officer. Earl Durham, governor general of the Canadas, had sent some insurgents, having acknowledged the fact of having used arms against government, to the island of Bermuda, under penalty of death, should they return. Lord Durham did it to save their lives, because they must otherwise have been executed. The measure was declared by the British law officers, to be illegal, because Bermuda did not belong to the governor-general's territory, he therefore could not bind the exiled to stay there ; besides, the insurgents had not been legally tried. Whereupon Lord Brougham brought in the Canada Government Indemnity bill, which declares the act of the earl illegal, but pronounces,

the Political Ethics I have spoken of the unconstitutionality and destructive tendency, to all substantial liberty, of a frequent travelling beyond the precise limits of a fundamental law, of constantly appealing to the first and original sovereign power, and upon 'the principles which preceded the laws, of building constructions to supersede them. Yet that which is dangerous cannot, on this account, be always avoided. This is true in common ethics; and not less so in political. The only safe way respecting conflicts and collisions, seems to us boldly to approach and investigate them, and to try to establish rules which shall guide us even in their mazes. The more perplexing a case, the greater the necessity to trace out its elementary, component parts and principles. Without this we shall be led to pedantry instead of truth. It is far easier indeed to establish

at the same time, his indemnity, and that of all officers having aided in it. The consequence was the resignation of Lord Durham. See his proclamation of Oct. 9, 1838, in which he gives his reasons for resigning, and his opinion of the indemnity bill.

Where there are written constitutions, above the whole legislature, the case, of course, is different. Nevertheless, laws of exception were passed in France under the elder Bourbons, after their restoration. The charter, as amended in 1830, says in article xiii., that the king has not the power either to suspend the laws themselves, or dispense with their execution.

Inasmuch as a bill of indemnity involves the supposition of a preceding illegal act, for which the ministers ask indemnity, none could be passed in America, for it would be suspending the constitution. If Congress take any notice of acts, considered by many as illegal, they can do nothing except declare by resolution, that the two houses hold them to be lawful, or, in the contrary case, impeach the respective officer.

CHAPTER III.—SECTION XIII. 81

a few general rules and pedantically to adhere to them, even in cases of conflicts, than to do what is essentially right and unequivocally true.

4. Extravagant construction is that which carries the effect of the text beyond its true limits, and, therefore, not any longer genuine construction, as the previous species becomes of a more and more doubtful character the more it approaches to this. The difference between the two is this, that the former remains, in spite of its transcendency, within the spirit of the law, or document to be construed; whilst extravagant construction abandons it. That the attempt, by mal-construction, to carry designs into the sphere of an instrument, amounts to the same with carrying the effect beyond its limits, is clear.

If the report to Charles X., king of France, made by the whole council of ministers, presided over by Prince Polignac, July 26, 1830, recommended to the king the annihilation of an essential part of the constitution, namely, the liberty of the press, guaranteed by article 8, of the charter; and founded this recommendation on the power, committed by the same charter to the king, of watching over the safety of the state, and the maintenance of that very charter which the ministers called a 'return to the constitution,' it was considered by the nation at large, as an extravagant construction of the fundamental law, and the 'July revolution' ensued, which not only overthrew the administration, but dethroned, likewise, the reigning family. The history of England, especially under the Stuarts, records many extravagant constructions, and instances are not wanting in the history of the United States.

Thus the very idea itself, of the state, has been extravagantly construed; for instance, when individuals were secretly despatched for, what was called, reasons of the state. Yet the chief idea, upon which the state is founded, is the safety of its members. From what we have said of the natural and essential character of power, it will naturally lean towards extravagant construction. It cannot help doing so, by its very nature.

CHAPTER IV.

Principles of sound Interpretation. — Genuineness of the Text. Falsified Texts in the highest as the lowest Spheres. — No Sentence of Words can have more than one True Sense. — Double Interpretation is false Interpretation. — Good Faith and Common Sense the leading Stars of all Genuine Interpretation. — Moral Obligation of Legal Counsel. — Lord Brougham's Opinion. — What Good Faith is in Interpretation. — Peculiar Circumstances which may make Subterfuges laudable. — Literal Interpretation an ever ready means of Tyranny. — Political Shuffling. — Words to be taken in their most probable sense. — Usus Loquendi. — To what it may relate. — Rules to ascertain the Meaning of doubtful Words. — 'Contemporanea expositio est fortissima in Lege.' — Instances. Technical Terms to be taken in their technical sense. — That which is inferior cannot defeat that which is superior. — The Text itself must furnish, if possible, the means of interpreting its own doubtful Words. — High Considerations on account of which we have to abandon Interpretation. — Case of Lord Bentink's Order in Council, abolishing Whipping of native Indian Soldiers, and a Sepoy and Drummer being lashed, because, having become a Christian, he was not entitled to the Privilege of Natives. — Care of Sir. Thomas Parkyns. — Recapitulation of the Principles of Interpretation.

I. We shall now examine the fundamental principles of every sort of interpretation, applied to whatever branch, to whatever text.

In the first place, interpretation must begin with what is likewise the first rule of criticism. We must convince ourselves that the text be genuine, that is, that it have proceeded from the utterer from whom it purports to have proceeded, or from whom others assert it to have proceeded; or that it belongs to that period, at which it is maintained that it originated. This is a rule of paramount importance in all departments, and not the least so in politics, whether it refer to documents issued by the highest authority, or to reports of speeches or conversational sayings, yet of a political character. Frauds of the most surprising character have been practised in altering and falsifying texts, or palming entirely spurious ones upon the public. They are daily committed as to letters and speeches, with flagrant boldness; laws have been interpolated, fictitious charters and decrees produced, wills materially changed, or spurious ones substituted, and grants of whole provinces fabricated.

The Isidorian Decretals, a collection of papal ordinances and resolutions of the councils of the church, first made by Isidore, archbishop of Seville, who died in 636, and afterwards enlarged in the ninth century, and many of which are of great importance respecting the papal government, have been proved to contain not a few spurious ones. So at least all protestants, and many catholics are convinced.

Luther declared that first of all he must be convinced of the genuineness of the bull issued against him, in 1519, before he could take any step, for it was well known, he said, with what brazen boldness papers had been produced in his time, said to have been issued under papal authority, which, nevertheless, proved to be spurious.

The emperor Napoleon proclaimed, in 1810, the concordate, which he was anxious to conclude with Pius VII, then retained at Fontainebleau, as having been finally ratified, and, consequently, henceforth to be observed, as law of the empire, while the pope declared it to be void, and not having been finally ratified.

During the late election struggle for the first parliament under Queen Victoria, a most arduous one between the whigs and tories, entire electioneering letters, purporting to have come from some of the highest persons in rank, went the rounds of all the papers, and nevertheless were soon after absolutely disavowed and declared, by their fictitious authors, to be, from beginning to end, base fabrications.

That reports of speeches, however honestly made, require this kind of criticism in a peculiarly high degree, is a matter of course.

II. No sentence, or form of words, can have more than one 'true sense,' and this only one we have to inquire for.

This is the very basis of all interpretation. Interpretation without it has no meaning. Every man or body of persons, making use of words, does so, in order to convey a certain meaning; and to find this precise meaning is the object of all interpretation. To have two meanings in view is equivalent to having no meaning—and amounts to absurdity. Even if a man use words, from kindness or malice, in such a way, that they may signify one or the other thing, according to the view of him to whom they are addressed, the utterer's meaning is not twofold; his meaning is simply not to express his opinion. Simple and clear as this position is, yet have men frequently abandoned it, and history gives us many accounts of melancholy effects in consequence. The wicked idea of mental reservation is chiefly founded upon the abandonment of this simple principle, nor has this simple principle been always acknowledged in law. In cases of slander, it was formerly held that the words spoken, admitted a double interpretation, the *asper* and the *mitis*. The former was used to interpret slanderous words of inferiors against superiors, of unprivileged against privileged persons, for instance, commoners against

CHAPTER IV.—SECTION II. 87

peers. And how *asper*, indeed, did the star-chamber make use of this deviation from common sense! And not only in cases of slander, but when a tailor had annoyed a peer by dunning him, when a commoner had said of a peer that he was no better man than himself. Had the principle been that the same words used against some persons are more punishable than against others, the case would have been different. This principle is acted upon every where. The Prussian code gives the right of disinheriting a child for having used bad names against the parent. Disrespectful words against a judge on the bench are far differently punished from what they would be if directed against him in common company. But the principle was actually that of double interpretation; in short, interpretation was mistaken for the act of bringing a sense *into* the words, instead of acknowledging as its sole legitimate office, that of bringing *the* sense *out* of them. It is this mistake alone which has actually produced with many persons so strong an aversion to the very word of interpretation.

The fictitious law case, composed by Pope and Fortescue, as having ensued in consequence of Sir John Swale having bequeathed to his friend, Mr. Straggling, "all my black and white horses," when there were found six black horses, six white ones, and six that were black and white, or pied horses, is certainly entertaining. Yet the question ought never to have arisen " whether the pied horses were included in the legacy," as was assumed by those gentlemen. As there can be but one meaning attached to any sentence, the testator could not have meant by his words all black and all white horses, and, at the same time, all black and white horses. The only difficulty arising from this will could be this; whether the testator meant to bequeath to Mr. Straggling all black and all white horses, *or* all black and white horses.

Nothing is more frequent, in tyrannical governments, than that the same law is made, according to the convenience of each single case, to mean all black and all white horses, and, at the same time, all black and white horses. Laws are made political see saws; for the indelible moral nature of men forces even a tyrant, to prefer, as long as possible, the protection of the law; nay, rather the mere pretence of protection by the letter, the very shadow of the law, to the bare and bold confession of power alone, as the sole basis of his demands.

III. In no case of human life, in which we are called upon to act, to apply rules or to understand what others say, can we dispense with common sense and good faith,[1] but they are peculiarly requisite in interpretation, because its object is to discover something that is doubtful, obscure, veiled; which, therefore, may admit of different explanations. If without common sense, we may make even of strict syllogism, an instrument, apparently, to prove absurdities, how much more are those two ingredients of all honesty necessary in interpretation. Common sense and good faith are the leading stars of all genuine interpretation. Be it repeated, our object is not to bend, twist, or shape the text, until at last we may succeed in forcing it into the mould of preconceived ideas, to extend or cut short in the manner of a Procrustes, but simply and solely to fix upon the true sense, whatever that may be.

It has been mentioned already, that the species of interpretation, which was called predestined, is, under certain circumstances, and with certain limits, allowed to be used by legal counsel. But they must take heed, that they do not injure, in doing so, the peace and safety of others. It would be absolutely immoral, if a counsel, by artful interpretation, were to throw plausible suspicion upon an innocent individual; that, however, which is absolutely immoral, cannot, under any circumstances, be ad-

---

(1) See Pol. Ethics, vol. i. book i. ch. 6.

missible. Knowingly to rob a person of lawful property by artful interpretation in favor of the client, will be declared by the conscience of every lawyer to be immoral. Yet to fix the precise limit between the demands of public justice in countries, in which it is believed that civil liberty depends in a great measure upon the fact that the court be entirely neutral, so long as the case is debating, and where it does not, therefore, direct the eliciting of the whole truth, even from the prisoner, and the grave duty of the counsel, to do every thing in favor of the client, on the one hand, and on the other hand, the stern demand that justice be done in reality, and not in appearance; that the innocent be not injured; that morality be not compromised; the fact that courts are established by society for society, for the sake of justice, not to be arenas for the dialectic skill of disputants — to fix the precise limit between these two grave demands of liberty and justice, is one of the most difficult subjects in the whole range of political ethics — a subject worthy of the highest and most fearless intellect, the purest honesty and humanity, and profoundest as well as most extensive learning. It is a subject, the philosophic treatment of which is more urgently asked for, the more civil liberty is extended; and the more undefined notions, in regard to forensic ethics, seem

CHAPTER IV.—SECTION III. 91

to be afloat; sometimes, actually, as if of all rational beings on the face of the globe, the advocate alone were absolved from all morality and ethic obligation. Though Lord Brougham, when he defended Queen Caroline, may have been urged to say far more in the warmth of pleading, than he would calmly maintain, it is, nevertheless, startling in the highest degree, if such a man dares to assert that 'an advocate, in the discharge of his duty, knows but one person in all the world, and that person is his client. To save that client by all means and expedients, and at all hazards and costs to other persons, and among them, to himself, is his first and only duty; and in performing this duty, he must not regard the alarm, the torments, the destruction, which he may bring upon others. Separating the duty of a patriot from that of an advocate, he must go on, reckless of consequences, though it should be his unhappy fate to involve his country in confusion.'[1]

If there be a person who does not see at once, how untenable this remark is, let him imagine, the

---

(1) Provided his speeches on that occasion are correctly reported in the Trial of the Queen of England, before the Peers of Great Britain, 2 vols. London, 1820. I do not know of a disavowal on the part of Lord Brougham; but if there exists one, should rejoice at its greater publicity. I repeat, that this remark may have been elicited by the cry of the tories, that the whigs used that occasion only to disturb the peace of England, a charge which came indeed with bad grace from those who had instituted the trial to satisfy the personal rancor of such a monarch as George IV., against their own conviction.

then Mr. Brougham had said, 'it is the duty of an advocate to save his client at all hazards, even should he bring shame upon his own mother.' And why is this more frightful than what Mr. Brougham actually asserted? In short, he forgot, as we are all so apt to do, the object, and remembered the means only. Justice is the object of trials, and, for the better obtaining it, it is thought that counsel on both sides should state all that can be said; but the object is not to save every person. If so, we should act very strangely to try the person at all. But although different duties may devolve upon different individuals, and continually do so, still the final object and ultimate duty remains the same. The lawyer does not cease to be a citizen, not cease to be a man, and all the fundamental obligations are the same for him as for all others. I doubt whether ever a bolder assertion has been made in the most fanatical periods respecting the obligations of propagating true religion, and extirpating heretics. The simple question, why? puts the whole assertion to naught. As to separating the duty of a patriot from that of advocate, it amounts to words, and words only. Moral obligations are eternal and immutable, though the acts which the same obligations require, may differ in different situations. If it is a duty to be patriotic at all, we can no where be absolved

CHAPTER IV.—SECTION IV. 93

from it, although patriotism may demand different acts, in time of war, from an only son, who supports aged persons and minor sisters, and from a son of a hale and healthy father, or a man who stands single in life.

IV. Good faith in interpretation means that we conscientiously desire to arrive at truth, that we honestly use all means to do so, and that we strictly adhere to it, when known to us — it means the shunning of subterfuges, quibbles and political shuffling — it means that we take the words fairly as they were meant.

Pope Sixtus IV. was bent on breaking down the Roman house of Colonna. He besieged the fortress of Marino, held by the Colonnas. One member of this family, the prothonotary Colonna, was a prisoner in the hands of the pope, who offered to give up the captive, if his family would surrender Marino. The offer was accepted, and the gates of the fortress were opened. On the other hand, the pope gave up the prothonotary, but — after having slain him. Alegretto Allegretti, Diari Sanesi, p. 817, gives the words of despair and the curse against the faith of the pope and all that thus shall keep their word, into which the mother of Colonna broke out, when she lifted up the severed head. The instance given by Vattel (B. II. ch. XVII. 273) is well known.

'Mahomed, Emperor of the Turks, at the taking of Negropont, having promised a man to spare his head, caused him to be cut in two through the middle of the body.'

Cardinal Bentivoglio, papal nuncio at Brussels, about the year 1614, considered the possession of the fortress of Wesel necessary, because it appeared to him, the 'Rhenish Geneva.' Spinola besieged it, and it had to surrender. The capitulation stipulated that one thousand Spaniards should be garrisoned in the place; he put three thousand into it. The citizens complained of the infringement of the capitulation, when Spinola answered, that the instrument did not express, that not more than a thousand soldiers should form the garrison.[1] Spinola was wrong, because his interpretation was not faithful, and he erred, besides, against another principle of interpretation, which will be stated farther below.

V. The character, however, of the transaction, to which the words, to be interpreted, relate, may be so peculiar that we cannot withhold our approbation from, or disown to be fair, what in other cases would be justly termed subterfuge.

German history gives a remarkable instance of this kind in the women of Weinsberg. After king

---

(1) Gaf, Hist. of the Synod of Dort; Ludolf, Theatre I, 491, both in German.

CHAPTER IV.—SECTION V.   95

Conrad had defeated, in 1140, Duke Guelf VI., in the battle of Weinsberg, this city was besieged, and soon reduced to the necessity of surrendering. The men were doomed to die. Upon this, the women implored Conrad to allow them, at least, to take away so much of their treasures as each could carry on her back. The request was granted; but when the appointed hour of their departure arrived, a long procession of women appeared, each carrying her husband. Duke Frederic, the king's brother, was enraged, but Conrad said: 'a royal word must not be twisted;' and the faithful wives were now allowed to carry away their *other* treasures likewise. Raumer's History of the Hohenstaufen, Vol. I. p. 397. Some hypercritics have doubted the fact, but, according to this distinguished historian, unreasonably so.

Here, the fact that the proposition came from the women, and that they made it purposely, in a manner that Conrad should be deceived, was decidedly against them, according to the principles of hermeneutics. There would not even be claimed for them the rule of construction, which gives the benefit of doubt to the weak, or makes us incline in doubtful cases toward mercy; because the truth was, that according to faithful interpretation there was no doubt whatever, as to the meaning in which the women had been desirous that Conrad should take the word treasure, in which he actually had taken it. Yet what generous soldier would not have granted them the full benefit of their praiseworthy subterfuge, and noble deception?

Lately a flute-player advertised in an English town, that, between the acts, he would exhibit the extraordinary feat of holding in his left hand a glass of wine, which he would drink, though the six strongest men of the place should hold his left arm and try to prevent him from bringing the glass with it to his lips. Six stout men accordingly grasped his arm at the night of performance, when he quietly advanced his right hand, took the glass, and quaffed the wine. Now, there are many countries in which 'tricking the public' is punishable. Some judicial proceeding might have been the consequence; but though the flute-player evidently resorted to a quibble, he must have been acquitted; because his advertisement showed to every intelligent man, that his words could not be meant to be taken in a plain sense. There is no reason why the man should not have the benefit of his wit, if the public choose to be gulled. They took the true ground in the above case, and applauded the ingenious deceiver.[1]

---

(1) We have seen already, chap. II. iv. how necessary common sense is, to make the commonest intercourse among men

CHAPTER IV.—SECTION VI.

VI. That artifice, to which revengeful tyranny so often resorts to obtain its objects, without incurring the direct charge of guilt, or to which a troubled conscience has recourse, to appease its remorse, when we are anxious to throw the guilt from our shoulders, in cases of divided responsibility, is generally, in its essence, founded upon literal or unfaithful interpretation.

After the infamous Jeffreys had done all in his power, during the trial, to ruin Algernon Sidney, he

---

a matter of possibility. Another instance is strikingly exhibited in the clown of the low comedy. The greater part of the jokes, by which these personages make the hearers laugh, rest on literal interpretation and the contrast between the sense which the spectator attaches to a sentence, and that in which the merry Andrew takes it. Almost the entire story of the far-famed Eulenspiegel is founded upon literal interpretation. Puns are generally nothing else. Nor does this contrast and surprise caused by it, belong to the lower sphere only; the finest wit, the sweetest passages, as well as the most majestic, of a Shakspeare, often turn upon it. That touching anecdote of Pope Gregory the Great, meeting with enslaved Angles in the market of Rome, and the conversion of the British to Christianity, which was caused by it, is founded upon literal interpretation. Palgrave, in his History of the Anglo-Saxons, relates it thus. Pope Gregory chanced to see some beautiful Saxon boys offered as slaves, and he asked: 'To what nation do these poor boys belong?' The dealer answered, 'They are Angles, Father.' 'Well may they be so called, for they are as comely as angels; and would that, like angels, they might become cherubim in heaven! But from which of the many provinces of Britain do they come?' 'From Deira, Father.' 'Indeed,' continued Gregory, speaking in Latin, 'De irâ Dei liberandi sunt.' And when, on asking the name of their king, he was told it was Ella, or Alla, he added, that 'Allelujah — praise ye the Lord — ought to be sung in his dominions.'

But the object of law and politics is neither to amuse or touch, and we must discard, therefore, literal interpretation.

declared, when pronouncing the sentence, that he had nothing to do with the matter, except to pronounce the law ;[1] the jury had decided that Sidney was guilty of treason; and no doubt, had he himself been brought to trial when James was expelled, would have used this as an argument for his defence.

The Spanish inquisition never sentenced a man to die, for the church seeks not the death of men; it only declared the culprits to be heretics, and handed them over to the secular authority. If thought necessary, the heretic was burnt, the officers of the inquisition being present. Yet, as late as about 1822, it was stoutly maintained that the inquisition had nothing whatsoever to do with the death of any heretic.[2]

In these cases of political shuffling, which extends into all branches of politics, the deed is represented as floating, as it were, between the actors; each one having performed but a part, is free of responsibility; as if two men might commit an act of for-

(1) See Sidney's Trial, in the Memoirs of his Life, in his Discourses on Government, &c. 4to ed.

(2) The title of the book I have forgotten, but its two arguments were, first, as I stated, that of political shuffling, and secondly, that the heretics in Spain were nearly all actual treators, politically speaking — alluding to the poor Moriscos. It is the view which Mr. Capefigue, in his ' Richelieu, Mazarin, la Fronde et Louis XIV,' Paris, 1835, 8 vols. seems to take. The only modern work of extent on the Spanish Inquisition, which deserves to be consulted as authority, is Llorente's History of the Inquisition.

gery between them, but each one remain not guilty of forgery, by doing an act, in itself and singly, lawful.

The memoirs of any man, who, high in power, is desirous of justifying reproachful acts, will always be found replete with this shuffling on the ground of literal interpretation, for instance, the late Memoirs of Godoy, the Prince of the Peace, who was so long the actual ruler of Spain, in the name of Charles IV.

VII. Faithful interpretation implies that words, or assemblages of words, be taken in that sense, which we honestly believe that their utterer attached to them. We have to take words, then, in their most probable sense, not in their original, etymological, or classical, if the text be such that we cannot fairly suppose the author used the words with skill, knowledge, and accurate care and selection. Grotius says: *si nulla sit conjectura quæ ducat alio, verba intelligenda sunt ex proprietate, non grammatica quæ est ex origine, sed populari ex usu. ' Quem penes arbitrium est et jus et norma loquendi.'* De Jure Bel. et Pac. Lib. II. c. XVI. II.[1]

---

(1) It is different, if our object is scientifically to settle which signification we ought to give to a word, if we write ourselves, not that which has been given by others, in common writing, or if we have to find out the signification a word had in former periods. In these cases, its etymology is frequently of much

VIII. According to the character of the text before us, we are obliged to take words, either in their common adaptation in daily life, or in the peculiar signification which they have in certain arts, sciences, sects, provinces, &c., in short, we have to take words according to what is termed *usus loquendi*. Horse, in common language, means a common animal; in a marine insurance case, it might mean this animal, or a certain part of the vessel; the connexion in which the word stands with others must give the decision. In a fire insurance case, the same word might have an architectural meaning. In a criminal case, it might mean a cloth horse used in laundries; and in a military order it might stand for the word cavalrist. If an officer had received an order to send 200 horse, and he were arraigned for disobedience, it would be an insufficient excuse were he to plead, that, the order being to send 200 horse,

importance; for if it does not unfold to us the entire and present signification of a word, the origin and history of a word will, nevertheless, shed considerable light upon its signification in many instances. Etymology becomes especially valuable in settling the precise meaning of synonymes. Altogether, etymology is one of the means of arriving at the signification of a word, and must be used as all the others, with common sense and in good faith. Archbishop Whately says: 'It is worth observing, as a striking instance of the little reliance to be placed on etymology as a guide to the meaning of a word (he ought to have said, absolute meaning; for etymology is in cases, no mean guide to the comparative meaning of a word), that Hypostasis, Substantia and Understanding, so widely different in their sense, correspond in their etymology.' Whately's Logic, Appendix ad verbum *Person*.

he did not know how to send them, since the men were not ordered at the same time. The word horse is frequently used in military language for a man with his horse. Thus the word soul stands frequently in statistical writings for individuals of the human species.

The general character of the text, whether it has emanated from a high or low source, and was drawn up with care or in haste, with a knowledge of the technical terms or not, the peculiar character of the author, and the especial connexion in which we find a doubtful word, must direct us in fixing upon a proper meaning.

IX. The *usus loquendi* may relate to a language in general, for instance, *femme sage* in French, which never means a wise woman but always a midwife—or *res* in Latin, which stands often for deeds—or *deed* in English, which stands often for a certain species of document. Or the *usus loquendi* may relate to a particular period, as *imperator*, which, at the time of the Roman republic, meant something different from what it signified during the empire; or the Greek πιστις which required a different meaning with the Christian writers. The word Obtaining means now frequently something entirely different from what it formerly did. Or it may relate to an individual author, thus Dion. Halicarnassus wrote on the idioms of Thucydides; or to a certain art or science, as we have seen above; or to a certain society, sect, &c.; or to a peculiar class in society, in a nation, for instance, the illiterate; or, finally, to a part of a country (*provincialisms*.)

X. The chief rules in ascertaining the meaning of doubtful words, besides the general one just given, that we are to take the words in that meaning which we may faithfully believe their utterer attached to them, (which word faithfully, however, does not imply our being carried away by personal feelings, violent dislikes, or conceited self-considerations,) are:

To try first to ascertain the meaning from other passages of the same text, in which the ambiguous word occurs, so used that it leaves no doubt—by parallels.

To ascertain it from other sources which we consider fully competent: thus, with regard to dead languages, from contemporary writers in the same language, or other contemporaries, who have chanced to explain the doubtful word, as Cicero explains several Greek words: with respect to living languages, from works or persons of the same nation, community, profession, art, &c., to which the doubtful word may relate, after these persons have established their character for competency and truth ; from previous expounders, of weighty authority, who are known to have paid much attention to the subject, and have done it with patience, learning, shrewdness, and conscientiousness; and from scholia, glosses, versions, and commentators.

To this rule refers the old maxim, acknowledged, among others by Lord Coke : ' Contemporanea expositio est fortissima in lege'—that is, as in all other cases, cum granu salis, as will appear more clearly from the sequel. We have in this particular, to guard ourselves against an inordinate veneration of old authors, merely because they are old, or against a too implicit reliance upon old authors, simply because they have been relied upon so long. Science advances, and it would be a matter of great regret, if successive centuries were unable to supersede by their labors some works of previous periods, though they have justly enjoyed, and for a long time, the reputation of authority. See especially the chapters on Precedents and Authorities.

We must be guided by the degree of care, which common sense will oblige us to believe to have been bestowed upon the selection of words and their arrangement. It would be in accordance with genuine interpretation, to take the same word in a wider or more restricted sense, or in an entirely different one, if we meet with it in an international treaty, from what we would do, had we the will of a private individual before us.

XI. The reader will find in this section, some instances, elucidating the preceding remarks.

In former ages, the students of the most frequented European universities were divided into various societies, called nations, which had their peculiar privileges, as there are to this day four 'nations' in the university of Glasgow. Property was not unfrequently bequeathed to them; the word nation, therefore, in a will containing such bequest, was to be taken in an entirely different sense from what would be given to it, in a national treaty. Again, the various tribes of the North American Indians are frequently called nations, and, secondly, the country they inhabit. In this peculiar signification, the word Nation is often used in public documents of the United States, relating to transactions with the Indians, for instance to their ceding of lands.

In the commercial treaties of the United States with other powers, the expression American goods is used. To give to this term the meaning of goods coming from any part of the continent of America, or its adjacent islands, would not be genuine interpretation.

CHAPTER IV. — SECTION XI. 105

The Tariff of the United States imposes a different duty upon manufactured articles of iron and on bar iron. A merchant in New York imported, in 1832, rolled iron, which the collector declared to be bar iron, liable to the heavier duty. The merchant claimed the benefit of the smaller duty, the imported article being, according to his opinion, manufactured iron. The question came before the proper court, in September of the same year, and witnesses, acquainted with the terms of the iron trade, were called to state whether the term manufactured iron applied to rolled iron or not. So, in another case, it was necessary to ascertain from credible persons, conversant with the subject, whether the term old iron was applicable to certain imported iron or not. Interesting, with regard to this subject, is likewise a case which attracted much attention, where it was decided by Mr. Justice Story, in the Circuit Court of the United States, that 'loaf sugar,' after being crushed, in which state it was imported into the United States, was not 'loaf sugar' within the Tariff Act of the United States of 1816. See United States v. Breed, 1 Sumner R. 159.

The constitution of Massachusetts provides that votes shall be given in writing. The proper officers, some years ago, had refused a printed vote, usually called a ticket. An action was consequently brought before the supreme court of that state, and it was decided that writing in this case included printing. See Henshaw v. Foster, Pick. R. 318. This can only be founded upon the principle that the *usus loquendi*, with regard to the word writing, has changed. There are, however, many who consider this interpretation decidedly what we have called an extravagant interpretation.

A will made in the state of New York, and providing means for the foundation of a common school, must be so interpreted that it means a school according to the standard of those, which are called common schools in that state, and not in Connecticut, Massachusetts, France, Prussia, or any other country.

If the late Mr. Girard, of Philadelphia, directs by his will, that at least two millions of dollars shall be used for the foundation of an asylum for 'poor male white orphans,' the word poor is to be interpreted according to the views of the community of the time in which he lived; while the word white every one knows is used to indicate the descendants of the Caucassian race, whose blood has remained unmixed with that of Negroes, Indians, or that of any other 'colored' race. The provision cannot be invalidated by the objection that no really white people exist. The word orphan must be taken in the sense

CHAPTER IV.—SECTION XI. 107

in which it is understood by nearly all nations, namely, meaning a fatherless child.

In a similar way have others left money for the foundation of schools for 'colored' people, meaning thereby negroes and mulattos. In some parts of the world, the term would signify people of mixed blood only, for instance, in the West Indies; while a court in New England would, perhaps, be obliged to include negroes, since this word, considered harsh, has given way, in a degree, to that of colored people, in that part of the Union. Again, if a testator should stipulate that a certain sum should be paid for the best chemical treatise on colorless blossoms, it would be sufficient to prove in court that colorless means green.

In September, 1837, a case of considerable importance was lately tried in England, in which the question was, whether a steam ship comes within the meaning of the act which regulates the London pilotage—an act passed when there were no steam vessels, claiming parliamentary attention.[1]

---

(1) My legal friends I trust will pardon me, if I quote here from the papers of the time, in lieu of better reference. The case came before Mr. Ballantine in the shape of an information against Capt. J. Anderson, master of the North Star steam-ship, who was charged with having, on the 14th of May last, acted as a pilot on board, after J. H. Bennett, a pilot duly licensed by the Trinity-house, had offered to take charge of the steamer; whereby the defendant had forfeited the sum of £15 16s. 9d., being double the amount of the sum which would have been demand-

If the testament of a Spaniard, or a law in Spain, makes use of the word christian, there can be no doubt that the judge is bound to take the term as synonymous with a christian who professes the Roman catholic religion; for the word *cristiano* is never taken in that country in any other sense. Suppose, however, the word christian is used in the United States, it would be against the rules of interpretation and good faith, to allow one sect to exclude another, on the ground, that the latter does not follow orthodox doctrines. Sects, in their zeal, may deprive each other of the name derived from the common founder of our religion, professed by all, and make specific points, *e. g.* a belief in the trinity, a test of the applicability of the name of a christian, but the interpreter would have no right to exclude unitarians as long as they call themselves christians, profess the bible, are enumerated by every statistical

able for the pilotage of the ship.—Mr Ballantine referred to the Act, and said he was of opinion that steamers ought to be exempt by the common sense of things. Pilots had to receive a certain education before they were licensed; but, however expert they might be in conducting sailing-vessels, it might require a different degree of skill to conduct a steam-vessel. A pilot superseded a master in the command of a ship, and the master of a steamer, it must be supposed, was appointed because he understood the nature of the engines and machinery. He did not understand how the new science was to be engrafted on the ancient custom. However expert a pilot might be as a seaman, he might be a very bad engineer. The complaint was then proved, and as the Act left the magistrate no discretion, the captain was fined in the penalty above stated and costs.

CHAPTER IV.—SECTION XI. 109

and geographical writer among the christian sects, and are considered as christians by every one in common life, whose judgment is not influenced by sectarian excitement. Theology has not to decide the point, if we have to interpret the word for purposes not lying within the province of divinity.

I do not know on what particular ground the judges of England decided the suit of the Attorney General of England, versus Shore, in July, 1834, according to which the management of an estate left some time ago by a lady Hewly, to be dispensed in relief to *christians*, was taken from Unitarians, as not coming within the meaning of the bequest, but if the decision was made merely on the ground that they do not believe in the Trinity, in the same manner as most other sects do, or as the established church does, it was a most startling decision, transgressing altogether the limits of legal interpretation, and would not fail to be soon overruled by act of parliament. If Unitarians are not christians, we must re-write ecclesiastic history. Perhaps it was strongly proved that the testator *did* mean to exclude the Unitarians, which, however, does not appear from the argument of Mr. Cooper.[1]

(1) Substance of the Speech of Charles Purton Cooper, in the suit of the Attorney General v. Shore, instituted in the High Court of Chancery, respecting Lady Hewley's Foundations, Wednesday, July 2, 1834, 2d edit. London, 1834.

I will give one more instance, which seems to me strikingly to illustrate some remarks which have been made above. Several acts of parliament regulate the lineal measure of G. Britain; the last of them, 5 George IV., c. 74, settles the length of a foot, in a manner that no doubt at any time can exist, by enacting the precise proportion which a yard is to bear to a pendulum vibrating seconds in the latitude of London. It is 36 inches to 39.1393. Clearer nothing can be. If an act of parliament, therefore, uses the terms yard, rod, furlong or mile, it would seem that no doubt as to their exact meaning can any longer exist. Yet the reform act declares that the residence of freemen, who have a right to vote at a place called Maldon, should be restricted to seven miles from the town hall. The important question arose: Are these seven miles to be measured by the road, or in a straight line over hedge and ditch? If the latter, fifty or sixty more voters belong to Maldon, and as matters stood during the election of 1837, a candidate would have obtained a seat in parliament, directly opposed to the one who must have been returned, if the other interpretation had been adopted.[1]

XII. If technical terms, belonging distinctly to the terminology of an art or science, are used as

---

(1) British Papers of October, 1837.

CHAPTER IV.—SECTION XII. 111

such, the same good faith demands that they must not be taken in their common but in their technical sense, as has been mentioned already.

Corresponding to this principle is this, that tropes be taken as tropes, and direct expressions as direct.

This principle, a deviation from which has caused great calamities, is generally of easy application in politics or law, yet not always. A clergyman who leaves a portion of his property ' for the greatest improvement of his flock,' will be understood to mean by flock the aggregate of his parishioners. A minister, however, convinced that no greater benefit could be bestowed upon his impoverished congregation than the improvement of their sheep, by importing a merino ram, had with great expense and infinite trouble, succeeded in obtaining one. For the last fifteen years he had bestowed the greatest care upon the improvement of his sheep to set a good example, and to assist his parishioners in improving theirs. When he died it was not easy for his executors, whom he directed by his will to use a considerable proportion of his property for the ' greatest improvement of his flock,'. to decide whether the testator had used the word in a tropic sense or not.

The previously mentioned instance of the New England farmer leaving a legacy for the benefit ' of the poor of the household of faith,' is likewise in point.

XIII. The special, particular and inferior, cannot defeat, or intentionally militate with the general and superior. If, therefore, we may attach two or more different meanings to a sentence, that is the true one which agrees most with the general and declared object of the text.

The late Mr. Girard specifies very minutely how his orphan asylum is to be built; but the architects have since declared that some of his directions cannot possibly be executed without great injury to the building, or danger to its inmates. It would be absurd to suppose that the testator was desirous of defeating the general object, i. e. the erection of an orphan asylum, by a specific direction, namely, that of architectural details, and consequently this portion of the will must be set aside, as of no effect.

When the particular, however, thus evidently defeats the general, whether in part or entirely, we have to resort to construction, in order to obviate the difficulty.

By way of exception, the specific may be contrary to the general, but it must not be forgotten, that exceptions are made on a ground still more general than the general object of the text; the rule, therefore, just given, is perfectly correct.

CHAPTER IV.—SECTION XIV.

The inferior officer has to obey the superior, but if the former is convinced that the latter is committing an act of treason, for instance, by manœuvering so that the troops or vessel must be taken or defeated, or by surrendering treacherously a fortress, or striking the flag without cause or avoiding fighting, when necessary, the inferior officer has the right to resist; or, in case of urgency, to kill him, when there is no other remedy in the midst of battle. Why? Because general safety is a law superior even to military or naval discipline.

XIV. Since our object is to discover the sense of the words before us, we must endeavor to arrive at it as much as possible from the words themselves, and bring to our assistance extraneous principles, rules, or any other aid, in that measure and degree, only as the strictest interpretation becomes difficult or impossible, (interpretation precedes construction) otherwise interpretation is liable to become predestined. Words have been used to express the sense, and through the words, if possible, we have to arrive at it.

Ernesti most solemnly warns against the belief in a perpetual and direct divine assistance in understanding the bible, without an unremitted zealous endeavor to arrive at the sense of the *words*, by the rules of sound interpretation. He calls it the abuse of reason, for by so doing we carry our opinion into the bible, and do not keep within the limits of the word, *i. e.* are unwilling to learn and receive the true meaning.

It is similar with those who have their own notions of public welfare, and carry them into a constitution, instead of faithfully interpreting the instrument. There are many individuals, with whom arguing upon public measures, or subjects of public interest, is out of the question, for speak to them about law, constitution, custom, interpretation, rules, or whatever you like, their invariable answer will be, what do I care for your letters! the people's welfare and plain common sense (by which, in this case, their own view is meant) are the only rules. They expect, by way of intuition, what the others expect by way of inspiration.

The more we apply to general principles, or opinions not expressed in the words, the less sure we can be, whether we understand the individual meaning of the text or not. The appeal to the motives of the utterers is, in most cases, doubtful, in many, dangerous; because it lies in the nature of things that it must be difficult, or impossible, to arrive at them otherwise than from the words themselves, except when a general declaration has taken place.

XV. Having said thus much, it becomes necessary to make a remark, which, perhaps more properly belongs to the subject of construction, but which may find a place to avoid apprehension. We have seen that interpretation means nothing more than finding out the true sense and meaning. But it is not said that interpretation is all that shall guide us, and although I believe the remarks in the next preceding section to be correct, still there are considerations, which ought to induce us to abandon interpretation, or with other words to sacrifice the direct meaning of a text to considerations still weightier ; especially not to slaughter justice, the sovereign object of laws, to the law itself, the means of obtaining it. In this respect, interpretation is much like political economy, a highly useful science, yet, withal, its object is to ascertain the laws which regulate the physical existence of society, and there are subjects superior to this. A war may not be advisable on simple grounds of political economy as to its nearest effects, and yet be urgently called for by all that is sacred to a nation, to mankind. This consideration is frequently forgotten by political economists, who, at times write, as if political economy had actually supplanted the science of natural law and politics.

The following case seems to me so interesting in its kind, that I feel warranted in stating it. When Lord Bentink was Governor General of India, he abolished flogging in the native army — may his name be honored! — not having authority to do the same in the British army in the East. If a sepoy professes the Christian religion, he thereby becomes subject to the British military laws proper, evidently to raise him. But this case happened, which was thus stated in a Madras paper.

'A few months ago the following case occurred in the Bengal army: — A Christian Sepoy deserted from his regiment, returned shortly afterwards, was tried by a court-martial, and sentenced to be corporally punished. The commanding officer thought himself prohibited from confirming the sentence by Lord W. Bentink's order abolishing corporal punishment in the native army. He referred the subject, however, for the opinion of the Judge Advocate General, who gave it as his opinion that the sentence was correct, and might be carried into effect, as the General Order of 24th February, 1835, does not extend to Christian drummers or musicians (to which prescribed trade the unfortunate individual happened to belong), and only affects native soldiers, *not professing the Christian religion.*'

Below, the reader will find the order of Lord

CHAPTER IV.—SECTION XV. 117

Bentink, and the interpretation of the Judge advocate general.[1] Now, even waving the important principle of sound construction, that in cases of doubt, that which is most lenient must be adopted, (see farther below,) and it was surely no stretch of the subject to consider it a matter of doubt, the Judge advocate general was wrong, because to be subject to English laws proper, was meant to be a benefit, and not to lead to the monstrosity that the profession of Christian religion should entitle the Sepoy to three hundred lashes, and defeat the other privilege which his darker color conferred upon him.

(1) 'Fort William, February 24, 1835.
'The Governor General of India in Council is pleased to direct, that the practice of punishing soldiers of the native army by the cat-o'nine tails or rattan, be discontinued at all the presidencies, and that it shall henceforth be competent to any regimental detachment, or brigade court-martial, to sentence a soldier of the native army to dismissal from the service, for any offence for which such soldier might now be punished by flogging, provided such sentence of dismissal shall not be carried into effect, unless confirmed by the general or other officer commanding the division.'

'Sir,— I have the honor to return the proceedings of an European court-martial, held in the 16th Native Infantry upon sepoy and musician John Dooming, received with your letter. I conceive that the prisoner Dooming was correctly sentenced to corporal punishment, and that Lieut. Colonel Tulloch might have carried the same into effect without any reference to you—the award not exceeding 300 lashes. The general order of 24th February, 1835, does not extend to Christian drummers or musicians, who are governed by the rules laid down in the Articles of War for the European troops. It only affects native soldiers not professing the Christian religion.

'G. Young, Judge Advocate General.
'16th April, 1836.'

Another interesting case in point is suggested by the trial of Sir William Parkyns for high treason in 1695, before Lord C. J. Holt, Lord C. J. Treby, and Mr. Justice Rokeby. He prayed to be allowed counsel, but was refused, because the Statute 7 Wm. III. ch. 3, allowing counsel to persons indicted for treason, did not go into effect, till the next day after that on which he was tried. It was in vain that the prisoner quoted a part of the preamble, which said that such an allowance was just and reasonable. The reply of Lord C. J. Holt was, that he must administer the law as he found it, and could not anticipate the operation of an act of parliament by even a single day. Whatever may be thought of the correctness of Lord Holt's decision in point of law, no doubt can be entertained, that humanity required him to postpone the trial for one day, and thus give the prisoner the benefit of the act. Sir William Parkyns was convicted and executed. See his case reported at length in the thirteenth volume of the State trials, Howell's Ed.

XVI. That which is probable, is preferable to the less probable; the fair, to the unfair; the customary, to the unusual; the easy, to the difficult; the intelligible, to the unintelligible.

We have to follow the special rules of interpretation, which have been given by proper authority.

Thus the Austrian code declares that the German is the original text, and shall be considered and referred to as such, in all interpretations and constructions of its translations into the several idioms spoken in the Austrian dominions.

We endeavor to find assistance in that which is near, before we proceed to that which is less so.

If we do not understand the word, we try whether its connexion in a sentence will shed light upon it; if we do not succeed, we endeavor to derive assistance from the period; if this be unavailing, we examine the whole instrument or work; if that leads us to no more satisfactory result, we examine other writings, &c., of the same author or authority; if that does not suffice, we resort to contemporaneous writers, or declarations, or laws similar to that which forms our text.

What we have said before includes the rule, that we are by no means bound to take an ambiguous word in that meaning, in which it may occur in another passage of the same text; for words, as is well known, have different meanings in different contexts.

XVII. In recapitulating the elementary principles of interpretation, we shall find the following.

1. A sentence, or form of words, can have but one true meaning.

2. There can be no sound interpretation without good faith and common sense.

3. Words are, therefore, to be taken as the utterer probably meant them to be taken. In doubtful cases, therefore, we take the customary signification, rather than the grammatical or classical; the technical rather than the etymological—*verba artis ex arte*—tropes as tropes. In general, the words are taken in that meaning, which agrees most with the character of both the text and the utterer.

4. The particular and inferior cannot defeat the general and superior.

5. The exception is founded upon the superior.

6. That which is probable, fair, and customary, is preferable to the improbable, unfair and unusual.

7. We follow special rules given by proper authority.

8. We endeavor to derive assistance from that which is more near, before proceeding to that which is less so.

9. Interpretation is not the object; but a means; hence superior considerations may exist.

This leads to construction.

CHAPTER V.

Construction is unavoidable.— The Causes why.—Instances.— Analogy or Parallelism the main Guide in Construing.—Rules of Construing. — We begin with that which is near. — Aim and Object of the Text. — Preambles of Laws. — Shall the Motives of the Utterer guide us?— How far?—'Lex Neminem cogit ad Impossibilia.'—Texts conferring Privileges. — Close construction necessary in construing Contracts.— Construction of Promises and Obligations. — Maximum and Minimum. — That which agrees most with the Spirit and Tenor of the Text is preferable. — Effects and Consequences of the Construction may guide us. — Blackstone.—Antiquity of Law makes frequently extensive Construction necessary. — Habitual close Interpretation and Construction favorable to Civil Liberty.— Words of a relative or generic Meaning to be taken in a relative or expansive Sense. — Rules respecting this Point. — The Weak have the Benefit of Doubt. — The Superior Object cannot be defeated by the Inferior. — Recapitulation of the Principles of Construction.

I. Construction is unavoidable. Men who use words, even with the best intent and great care as well as skill, cannot foresee all possible complex cases, and if they could, they would be unable to provide for them, for each complex case would require its own provision and rule; times and relations change, so that after a long lapse of time, we must either give up the letter of the law, or its intent, since both, owing to a change in circumstances, do not any longer agree. If, with all imaginable wisdom in the utterer, construction becomes thus necessary, it is still more so the case, from other circumstances. Interpretation, seeking but for the true sense, forsakes us, when the text is no longer *directly* applicable, because the utterer, not foreseeing this case, did not mean it, therefore it has no true sense in this particular case.

By the charter of appointment of the hereditary lord high chamberlain of England, he has a right to the dress worn by the monarch at each coronation in which the officer is to appear on the first court after that ceremony. The present monarch is a queen; was the officer to appear in her majesty's dress? This instance has been taken, on account of the glaring absurdity to which interpretation would have led; or, rather, interpretation was not necessary, because there is no dubious sense at all. The framer of the charter did not think of the case of a queen's coronation. The instrument itself, therefore, expresses nothing in regard to this case; for impossible things are nowhere to be supposed; and there are very many things impossible, though not physically impossible. It was impossible for the

CHAPTER V.—SECTION I. 123

lord high chamberlain to appear in petticoats. Ludicrous as this instance seems, there are many others touching subjects of the highest importance, which are equally strong in their character.

It appeared in a case in London, in October, 1837, that there are five hundred acts relating to turnpikes and roads, many of which affect the jurisdiction over them, and clash most seriously. Interpretation cannot lead us out of such mazes.

A cotemporary periodical made, not long ago, the following remark, respecting property left for public purposes, especially for schools, and other institutions for education, if they prescribe particulars relating solely to the period of the foundation.[1]

' An adherence to original rules, when such rules are no longer applicable, owing to change of circumstances, is, in effect to defeat the will of the testator. In the instance of private property, an individual, by a rule of law, called the rule against perpetuities, is not allowed to fetter an inheritance beyond a life or lives in being, and twenty-one years afterwards; the average of which time has been calculated to amount to 70 years. For a longer time than this it cannot be conceived that the circumstances of a family can be foreseen; and, for this

(1) London Quarterly Journal of Education, No. XIX, article on Lieber's Girard Report.

reason, the law gives the power to the individual in possession at the expiration of that period, to re-model the limitations of the property to suit the altered position of the family in society. Following this example, might not some very salutary regulations be laid down with regard to property given for public purposes. Nothing can be more absurd, than to adhere to the letter.'

I proceed now, to the general principles of construction.

II. All principles of interpretation, at all applicable to construction, according to its definition, are good and valid also, with regard to construction, for the same reasons that they hold in interpretation.

The main aid and guide of construction is, as has been stated already, analogy; understanding the term as explained in chapter iii, iii, or rather, parallelism. Following a similar principle to that given in chap. iv, xiv, we shall find that in use of parallelism, we have carefully to begin with that which is near, and proceed to that which is less so, according only, as we find ourselves unable to construe, without seeking means in a wider circle.

If we have to construe part of a speech, will, law, or constitution, we ought first to inquire whether we can construe it by way of analogy from the same

CHAPTER V.—SECTION II. 125

speech, will, law, or constitution; if not, whether there are similar acts, &c., which have proceeded from the same authority. If we have to construe commentaries, we have to try first whether we can draw any assistance from the commentaries or glosses of the same author, before we proceed to those of another; and before we seek for assistance in the whole literature, we ought to examine the commentators and writers of the same period. So the theologian, in order to interpret or construe a sentence of Paul, must first inquire, whether he can explain it from other parts of Paul's writings; if not, he must then inquire whether he can find assistance in other writings of the new testament, and so on.

There may exist, of course, some reasons, why the interpreter or constructor should omit these links, as he would be obliged to do in cases where Paul quotes passages of the old testament, or uses words, which have reference to the customs or rites of Greek paganism.[1]

The Austrian civil code, introduction, 7, gives this rule:

'If a legal case cannot be decided, either by the words, or the natural sense of a law, it is necessary

---

(1) See Ernesti Institutio, parts I. and II. and his commentators, Ammon, Stuart, Terrot, &c., and Horne's introduction to the Critical Study of the Scriptures, vol. II. part II. Book II. Section I. and *seq.*

to refer to similar cases distinctly decided by the laws, (in this code,) and to the reasons of other laws akin to the doubtful case. If the case still remains doubtful, it must be decided according to the principles of natural law, applied to the carefully collected and maturely weighed circumstances.' We have here the gradual extension of construction in concentric circles distinctly prescribed. See, also, the French civil code, 1161.

III. In conformity with the primary rule, which directs us to proceed from that which is near, to that which is less so, we have likewise to inquire first as to the aim and object of the text, before we apply to more general rules, reasons, or arguments; and as it is frequently impossible to learn the object of a law more clearly than by an inquiry into the causes which lead to its being issued, a knowledge of these causes is of the highest importance. See 1 Blackstone, 59. Indeed, the general principle, that any thing, which we are desirous clearly to understand, must be taken with all its adjuncts — a principle of peculiar importance respecting precedents — would demand the rule just given.

The Prussian code, introduction, 46, says: 'in deciding upon dubious cases, the judge is not allowed to substitute any other meaning for the laws than that which clearly appears from the words, their

CHAPTER V.—SECTION IV. 127

connection, with reference to the doubtful subject, or from the *next and undoubted* reason of the law.[1]

This is the reason why Mr. Bentham, in his Principles of Legislation, advises that no law should be passed without a proper preamble, stating the reasons and causes of the law. Still, preambles cannot altogether supersede construction, inasmuch as they themselves must necessarily be sometimes subject to construction or interpretation. Such as the preambles have been so far, they are not always safe guides, nor are the titles of laws. See 1 Kent's Commentaries, section XX. p. 460, and sequel.

IV. We have seen already, that, in many cases, it is difficult to discover the motives, which may have prompted those who drew up the text; but it is also dangerous to construe upon supposed motives, if they are not plainly expressed. Every one is apt to substitute what his motives would have been, or perhaps, unconsciously, to fashion the supposed

---

(1) If I quote frequently from the Prussian code, and, perhaps, more so than from any other code of the European continent, it is simply because it is a fact, that far more patience has been bestowed upon it, in devising it, whatever may be our opinion of some of its details. The remarks of Mr. de Savigny in his work, 'On the Aptitude of the present Age for Legislation and Jurisprudence,' translated by A. Hayward, Esq., of Lincoln's Inn, on the history of this code, the long time spent in maturing it, and a variety of means resorted to in order to perfect it, are worthy of perusal, though we do not agree with Mr. de Savigny on the main points, as to the subject of his work.

motives according to his own interests and views of the case ; and nothing is a more ready means to bend laws, charters, wills, treaties, &c., according to preconceived purposes, than by their construction upon supposed motives. To be brief, unless motives are expressed, it is exceedingly difficult to find them out, except by the text itself; they must form, therefore, in most cases, a subject to be found out by the text, not the ground on which we construe it.

The Prussian code distinctly declares, respecting privileges, that, 'in doubtful cases, reference shall be had rather to the proper contents of the privilege (*i. e.* the instrument granting it) than to the motives specified in the first grant of the same.' Introduction, Of Laws in General, 58.

V. No law, will, or whatever the document may be, which forms the text, can be understood to demand impossible things. If a provision, or part of it, directly does so, that part is void, and not on that account the whole. 'Lex neminem cogit ad impossibilia.'

A short time ago, the Legislature of South Carolina passed an act incorporating a bank, in which the day, when the subscription books were to be opened, and that on which they were to be closed, was fixed. Before the act, however, finally passed, an amendment was made, which fixed the day on which the books were to be opened, beyond that on which they were to be closed, without altering the latter. The act passed in this state, in the press of business. Similar mistakes have happened in England.

VI. Whenever the text, to be interpreted, bestows privileges upon one or some persons, (to the exclusion, therefore, of others) ambiguous parts are always to be construed in favor of the non-privileged, provided the object of the privilege be not thereby defeated.

The commonest principle of fairness dictates the former; common sense, the latter. Those who are privileged are not farther to be favored than the instrument, granting the privilege, distinctly indicates. If a favor, or privilege, has been granted, in consideration of some service done, or to be done, they must be considered as equivalents, and the matter as settled.

In addition to English commentaries on this subject, we mention here the Prussian code, introduction, 54, 'privileges and exemptions must be construed, in doubtful cases, so as to be least injurious to the third (i. e. the non-privileged) person.' The civil code directs the same.

VII. The more the text partakes of the character of a compact, the more necessary becomes close construction; for the compact must be acknowledged as the true and sole ground of agreement; and the nature of the text obliges us to presume that much care has been bestowed upon the selection of words; still, if a word, or sentence of a contract, leaves a decided doubt, sound sense dictates that they are to be taken most strongly against the party using it; because it was his affair to word the instrument well: '*Verba ambigua fortius accipiuntur contra proferentem.*' The civil law acknowledges the same principle: '*In obscuris quod minimum est, sequimur, secundum promissorem interpretamur.*' Dig. L. 50, Tit. 17, 1. 9, 58, 96.

VIII. Whenever the text expresses the promise or obligation of performing some act, the demand contained in the text is to be taken as the minimum, if it involves a sacrifice of the performer and a benefit of the person towards whom the act is to be performed; but as the maximum, if the performance of the act is to the advantage of the performer, and the disadvantage of the other party.

Good faith and common sense are sufficient to show the justice of this rule highly important, as

CHAPTER V.—SECTION VIII.

the disregard of it is contrary to these first elements of all interpretation, and defeat the objects of any text of the above charter.

A leaves a large fortune to B, on condition to pay annually the sum of £500 to a hospital; in case of failure, C shall come in as heir and have half of the property. B is of a peculiarly benevolent disposition, and pays £1000 instead of £500 to the hospital. C brings in an action, claiming half of the fortune, on the ground that B has not strictly complied with the terms of A's will. The judge would be obliged to decide that there is no ground for the action, because, in this case, the minor, £500, is contained in the major, £1000. B has performed his obligation, and done something over and above it. The sum of £500, mentioned in the will, is the minimum, because its payment is a sacrifice to B, and a benefit to the hospital.

The case, related above, when Spinola was to garrison one thousand men in Wesel, according to the articles of surrender, and on complaint that he had sent in more, pleaded that he complied with the articles, because he had sent one thousand men, and that the said articles did not stipulate, that he should not garrison more than one thousand in Wesel, is likewise in point.

It was faithless and against common sense in Spinola to interpret thus; the capitulation expressed the maximum, because the performance of the act was beneficial to him, and exacted a sacrifice on the part of the citizens. Indeed, the number of the soldiers to be quartered in Wesel, of itself was of no importance; it was the support they required, and their military importance with regard to the prosecution of the war, which made the capitulation desirable. The citizens of Wesel would have had no right to complain had Spinola quartered with them 800 men only; but the case would have changed had the 1000 men been demanded, on account of security, for instance, or that they might have an excuse for surrendering, by showing his strength.

If, however, the service to be performed, and stipulated for, is of a kind that, if the measure agreed upon be exceeded, it becomes an injury, good faith and common sense oblige us to consider the stipulation a maximum. To many readers, all these remarks may appear superfluous; yet have violations of these elementary rules taken place so often, in order to rob people of their property, that it is right we should clearly present them to our mind. Respecting the last rule, I instance a case in which A was obliged to let B have sufficient water from a dyke, to drive B's mill. It was stipulated that a certain flood gate should not be closed. In consequence of a dispute, A opened two instead of one, and destroyed much of B's property, maintaining that he had complied with the contract.

IX. As we are bound to prefer that which is fair to that which is less so, if the mere words of the text may mean one or the other, so we are bound to prefer in construction that which agrees most with the substance of the text.

1 Blackstone, 60, French civil code, 1158; Pufendorf, Law of Nature and Nations, Book V. 12. Grotius as quoted above.

X. The effect and consequences may frequently guide us in construction, but with the same caution which we recommended with regard to deriving assistance from the motives of the utterer; for people imagine very different effects to ensue from the same causes, and again, they have very different opinions respecting the beneficial tendency of the same effect.

See 1 Blackstone, 59; 1 Kent's Commentaries, Sect. xx. 460, and sequel.

Though I shall touch upon the subject of the construction of laws separately, I will give here

Blackstone's words respecting it; because they are applicable in a wider circle than merely to laws. He says, 1. 59,—' The fairest and most rational method to interpret the will of the legislator, is by exploring his intentions at a time when the law was made, by *signs*, the most natural and probable. And these signs are either the words, the context, the subject-matter, the effects and consequence, or the spirit and reason of the law.'

I have never been able to understand how the subject-matter, effects, &c., can be called signs. Pufendorf has been justly followed by Blackstone on this subject, and the words of the former are; ' Signa illa sunt duum generum, verba, et aliæ conjecturæ; quæ considerantur aut seorsim aut conjunctim.' De Jure N. et G. v. cap. xii. 2. But the word *sign* must be taken here in the peculiar sense which Pufendorf defines in the work itself.

XI. The farther removed the time of the origin of any text may be from us, the more we are at times authorized or bound, as the case may be, to resort to extensive construction. For times and the relations of things change, and if the laws, &c., do not change accordingly, to effect which is rarely in the power of the construer, they must be applied according to the altered circumstances, if they shall continue to mean sense or to remain beneficial. The benefit of the community is the supreme law, and however frequently this may have been abused, and is daily abusing, it is nevertheless true. Whether we rejoice in it or not, the world moves on, and no man can run against the movement of his time. Laws must be understood to mean something for the advantage of society; and if obsolete laws are not abolished by the proper authority, practical life itself, that is, the people, will and must abolish them, or alter them in their application; even a Mansfield was obliged to charge the jury, in some cases, to find the value of stolen articles under forty shillings, when the real and evident value was far higher.

Great evil has arisen at various epochs from insisting on established laws in times of great crisis; as if the human mind could be permanently fettered by laws of by-gone generations. It was the misfortune of the catholic party, at the time of the reformation, that they did not understand the regenerating spirit of Europe, and thought they could conjure it by the formulas of ancient laws. Neither the papal excommunication, nor the canon law, was able to banish or encircle this spirit. Previous to almost every revolution, there exists a party whose characteristic trait is this mistake.

A single glance at the book on the State in the Political Ethics will suffice, I trust, to protect me against any imputation that I do not sufficiently value the supremacy of the law. I consider it all important.

XII. Yet it is necessary to remember well, that in general, nothing is so favorable to that great essential of all civil liberty—the protection of individual rights, as close interpretation and construction. Most laws lose in their protective power, in the common intercourse of men, (which is the most important, because of daily and hourly occurrence,) according as they are loosely interpreted. Several surprising decisions of the English courts exist, indeed, which were the consequence of an apparently literal interpretation. Verdicts even are not wanting, which evidently defeated the object of the law, in consequence of adhering to its mere letter; yet I do not hesitate to avow my firm belief that England owes her civil liberty, and that civic spirit, so common in the whole country, compared to many others, to no circumstance in a higher degree than to the habitually close construction of her laws. On the other hand, the laws of the European continent were, for a long time, loosely interpreted, and construed according to the effects and presumed motives of the legislator, &c., whenever there was a question of right between the individual and those who possessed the power, or the same law was differently interpreted on different occasions.

The result of our considerations then will be, that we ought to adhere to close construction, as long as we can; but we must not forget that the 'letter killeth,' and an enlarged construction becomes necessary, when the relations of things enlarge or change. We ought to be careful, however, not to misjudge our own times; for every one, who is desirous of justifying an extravagant construction, does it on the ground, that the case is of a peculiar character and the present time a crisis. Every demagogue, tyrant, or selfish man, in public or private life, resorts to this argument, to palliate unwarranted acts before others, or his own conscience. However delicate this subject may be, the truth of what has been said is nevertheless apparent; and, to be safe in this particular, we must return to one of the first principles, that, without good faith and conscientiousness, there is no true interpretation or construction possible.

XIII. Words of a relative or of a generic meaning must be taken in a relative or expansive sense, if the character and object of the text oblige us to do so, but not if they have been used to express something definite or absolute.

If the term 'genteel education' is used with reference to the character of a school to be supported by certain foundations, it will be found necessary to take the expression in that meaning, which every successive period attaches to it. If the direction, however, is to instruct in certain branches which have been enumerated, and it were then added: and 'all branches called a genteel education,' there might be reason to limit the meaning to that of the time.

The lawmakers cannot have had Mr. Perkins's steam-gun in view specifically, if they passed the law, relating to murderous arms, previous to the invention of the steam-gun; yet the word arms necessarily includes this species, because the steam-gun agrees in all essentials with the other arms specifically mentioned in that law.

'A suit of clothes' means (in the United States) something very different from what it did formerly, or does at present, in other countries. A judge, in the state of Kentucky, decided that a suit of clothes to be given, according to stipulation, to an apprentice, after having served his time, ought to be worth forty dollars.

CHAPTER V.—SECTION XIII.

It has been considered that the charter of Harvard University, when making use of the term 'christian doctrine,' applies as well to unitarians as trinitarians; though no unitarians were existing in New England, when the charter was granted.

It is necessary to pay attention to three points in questions of this character:

First. Did the utterer use the doubtful word in a definite, absolute, or circumscribed meaning; or did he make use of the word as a relative, generic, or expansive term.

Secondly, if the latter be the case, what did the utterer consider as an absolute and definitely characteristic, or as a generic sign: what may be considered in that which is designated by a certain word, as fixed and unalterable, and what as variable, expansive, or contractive, according to the change of circumstances and relations between things and men.

Thirdly, is the subject to which the text relates of that elementary, vital, and absorbing importance to society, that every other interest, or consideration, must yield; so that in construing the difficult parts of the text, we are obliged to regulate our decision rather by the meaning which the words would now have, considering things and circumstances as they now exist, than by the known meaning which the utterer attached to them, considering the then relations. Here the difference between interpretation and construction is evident.

The many foundations, which were made before the time of the reformation for the support of clergymen, or the diffusion of christianity by other means, were construed by the protestants to mean, that the pious founders were anxious to diffuse true religion, and that at the time of the reformation they would have meant biblical or evangelical christianity, or whatever else it may be called. Interpretation cannot but acknowledge that the founders had distinctly and positively the Roman apostolic catholic religion in view. They neither thought of protestantism, nor would they have viewed its doctrines, at their time, with any thing else than aversion.

Yet religion is too important to allow any generation to forestall every future change. What were the catholic priests to do, when the people had become protestant?

The conversion of funds, left for the reading of masses for the dead, into school funds, was not in consequence of any transcendant construction. This was an absolute change, which could only take place in consequence of high legislative action. When, on the other hand, individuals, who united in their capacity the character of priest and sovereign, and who had been elected on the very ground, that they were catholic priests, and, consequently, not married, embraced protestantism without resigning, but, on the contrary, declaring themselves hereditary princes, after having married, it was revolution, and can be judged of only on that ground.[1]

XIV. Whenever a decision between the powerful and the weak depends upon our construction, the benefit of the doubt is given to the weak. Our construction must of course not defeat the general object of the text.

This principle has always been acknowledged, though it has not always prevailed. When the elector of Saxony demanded that Luther should be called to the diet, assembled at Worms, and be heard, the elector urged that it is customary according to German liberty, to prefer, in doubtful cases, the lenient one.[2]

XV. The general and superior object cannot be defeated by a less general and inferior direction;

---

(1) Prince Albert of Prussia, the master of the Teutonic order, thus made himself duke of Prussia by revolution alone; and it was revolution, which Luther advised some prelates to resort to, when he called upon them to profess protestantism and declare themselves independent sovereigns. No construction whatever could arrive at this decision; but revolutions become at times indispensable; this, however, is not the place to discuss the subject.

(2) Palavicinus, I. 26, 5.

and, in general, the higher prevails over the lower, the principle over a specific direction.

Pufendorf gives, to illustrate another rule, however, the instance, that there exists a law that no citizen shall carry arms on festivals; another to assemble with arms, as soon as the alarm bell is sounded. A hostile fleet appears on Sunday off the harbor, the bells are rung, what has the citizen to do? He has to go armed of course, because the first mentioned law was given to maintain peace and safety; the second, to save the city. The repelling of the enemy, and the freedom of the city, is the most important. It does not appear to me, that in this case the citizen ought to go armed on Sunday, ' because the second law forms an exception to the first,' or if it does, it is only because the exception is founded upon a more general principle; if it were not, it could not possibly have the power of overcoming the other law, which prohibits going armed on festival days.

If the exceptions are specified, or if we can give to a text the character of an exception to the general, the exception of course prevails as we have stated.

XVI. In order to give the proper meaning to each word or sentence, we ought to consider the whole text or discourse together; without it, we can never arrive at a fair interpretation or construction.

XVII. Recapitulating the general principles of construction, we shall find the following to be most essential points:

1. All principles of interpretation, if at all applicable to construction, are valid for the latter.

2. The main guide of construction is analogy, or rather reasoning by parallelism.

3. The aim and object of an instrument, law, &c., are essential, if distinctly known, in construing them.

4. So also may be the causes of a law.

5. No text imposing obligations is understood to demand impossible things.

6. Privileges, or favors, are to be construed so as to be least injurious to the non-privileged or unfavored.

7. The more the text partakes of the nature of a compact, or solemn agreement, the closer ought to be its construction.

8. A text imposing a performance, expresses the minimum, if the performance is a sacrifice to the performer, the maximum, if it involves a sacrifice or sufferance on the side of the other party.

9. The construction ought to harmonize with the substance and general spirit of the text.

10. The effects, which would result from one or the other construction, may guide us in deciding which construction we ought to adopt.

11. The older a law, or any text containing regulations of our actions, though given long ago, the more extensive the construction must be in certain cases.

12. Yet nothing contributes more to the substantial protection of individual liberty, than a habitually close interpretation and construction.

13. It is important to ascertain, whether words were used in a definite, absolute, and circumscribed meaning, or in a generic, relative, or expansive character.

14. Let the weak have the benefit of a doubt, without defeating the general object of the law. Let mercy prevail if there be real doubt.

15. A consideration of the entire text or discourse is necessary, in order to construe fairly and faithfully.

16. Above all, be faithful in all construction. Construction is the building up with given elements, not the forcing of extraneous matter into a text.

CHAPTER VI.

Hermeneutic Rules respecting Detached spoken Words or Sentences. — Conversation. — Hearsay. — In judicial Procedures. Letters, Journals, Private Notes. — Speeches. — Pamphlets. — Orders, Directions, &c. of a passing Nature. — Contracts, Deeds, Wills, &c. — Laws must at times be interpreted or construed. — Hermeneutic Rules respecting Laws. — Constitutions. — Constitutions are Laws and Guarantees. — Various Constitutions. — Rules of Constitutional Hermeneutics. — The Veto and pardoning Privilege. — International Treaties.

I. If we apply these general rules of interpretation and construction, to the various subjects, which, in politics and law, may form the text, some particular rules peculiar to these respective subjects, or of especial importance respecting one or the other will be found.

II. *Detached spoken words or sentences*, not pronounced on solemn occasions, or in public. Merely spoken words may be of the greatest importance, for instance, in criminal cases. Every thing may depend upon a proper understanding of some words uttered by a person; or they may possess very high political importance; for instance, the answer which queen Elizabeth gave, when asked whom she designated as the fittest person to succeed her.

The more the discourse, in which the words in question were uttered, assumes the character of conversation, the less importance we can attach to them; for, to understand them entirely, we ought to know the accent, the gesture, the expression of the face, which accompanied them, or the whole spirit of the conversation, which gave rise to them. This spirit of the conversation, or the expression of the features during the utterance, may indicate, indeed, that the very contrary, by way of jest or irony, was meant from what the words directly would intimate. The accent of speech, and that which prevails as the general idea in the minds of the utterer and hearer, are in all conversations or spoken words, not only sufficient substitutes for exactly grammatical use of pronouns and relatives, but in many cases, better and clearer. Written words allow of calm perusal and considerate application of each pronoun, to its proper noun. Wherever tyranny sends out her listening informers, it will be found that many people are sentenced, because not sufficient or no regard is paid to these concomitants of all conversational intercourse.

All these accompaniments of oral intercourse are, however, evanescent; the words alone are repeated, and these undergo considerable changes with each new transmission. The frailty of tradition shows itself no where more strongly than in hear-say, and reports are never more to be dreaded than when relating to subjects, which are transmitted in secret. Woe to the man who lends his ear to whispers! Woe to him who is influenced by, what is commonly called talk, be this ultimately transmitted orally, or in newspapers or memoirs. We may lay it down, then, as a rule, to discard them altogether, unless they have reference to facts, which facts we have it in our power to ascertain otherwise. It is a very simple rule, yet daily forgotten, in common intercourse, in newspaper debates, in politics, be they of a popular sort or relating to courts, in judicial trials, and in the study of history. If you peruse a file of papers, issued during the wars between England and France under Napoleon, you will find striking and incredible proofs of the remark just made. If the above-mentioned rule were strictly adhered to, it would give a death-blow, at once, to all systems of espionage.

In judging by hear-say, people are always too apt to break two necessary and obvious rules; the one furnished by criticism, the other by common morality. The first has been mentioned already, namely, inquire first of all, whether the text be genuine. Were the words really uttered? Were they uttered precisely so? Were they not uttered under circumstances which made them convey an entirely different meaning from what they seem to express in their detached form, as reported? The second, furnished by common morality, is, that we should not studiously endeavor to make the worst of the words or actions of our neighbors. Plain justice demands that we should take them in the spirit in which they were meant, and that we should endeavor to find out that spirit; plain charity demands that we should give full weight to a possible good interpretation, which charity becomes but justice, considering that all of us stand in equal need of it. Now, read the papers, especially if any question of vital interest is pending, be it in politics or religion, or whatever other sphere, and it will be seen whether it is worth while to mention two rules, which, in themselves seem so plain, that no one might be supposed to dissent from them.

In judicial procedures, it will be probably found a safe rule to disregard and discard at once, any report of words, which may involve the injury of any one, and, at the same time, require interpretation at all. If, however, the adoption of the words injures one party, and the discarding, another, it is necessary, of course, to proceed in good faith upon all the sound rules of interpretation and construction. This is frequently of great importance respecting the last declarations of persons on their death-bed. In these cases, good faith obliges us, not to found any argument upon the nice position of words, or the peculiar reference which certain pronouns may have; because, as has been alluded to already, even in common converse, we refer pronouns much more to the logical subject of the sentence, than to the grammatical, because the former is uppermost in our mind. Every one who has ever written for the press, will have found that he has to change, after a careful perusal of what he wrote with vivid interest, these pronouns, which in the original draft related to the general subject, rather than to the subject of the specific sentence. The same happens with the singular and plural number of nouns and verbs.

There is a remarkable instance, illustrating this subject, on record, in the trial of Earl Strafford for high treason. I mean the deposition of Sir Henry Vane respecting the notes which his father had taken of a debate at the council-table of Charles I. In these, Strafford was made to say, among other things: 'And you, (the king) have an army in Ireland, that you may employ to reduce this kingdom to obedience; for I am confident the Scots cannot hold out five months;' upon which the question arose, whether Strafford used *this, that* or *their*, and whether this meant England or Scotland.[1]

III. *Letters, Journals, private Notes, &c.*

This is not the place to discuss the outrage of the unauthorized publishing of private letters, or the crime of unauthorized opening them. A letter thief, as Luther calls every one, officer or not, who breaks the seal of a letter not addressed to him, is as bad, and, at times, worse, than a common thief, according to the same authority; and Lord Falkland, even in those troubled times in which he lived, declared the opener of letters to be the worst of spies. Clarendon, VI. 235.

The unauthorised opening of private letters, or perusing notes for private use only, is a most immoral act, well known and felt by every 'letter thief;' for, who will boldly and without blushing, acknowledge it. It is breaking into one of the most sacred sanctuaries of humanity. Nearly the same rule applies to the unauthorized publication of private letters, even though they may have been directed to us. Letters do not become absolutely ours,

(1) See State Trials, vol. III. p. 1442. Brodie's History of the British Empire, Edinb. 1822, vol. III. p. 91. Also Lingard, vol. X. chap. II. Lingard, however, is not important as to this part of British history.

that is, we are not absolutely free to dispose of their contents, although the letters be directed to us. The American law acknowledges this; it has been decided, that the law, that no person has the right of publishing any thing of another without a written order or permission of the writer, is applicable to letters; the property of them remains in the letter-writer.

Still, letters are not unfrequently published, sometimes with, sometimes without, the consent of the author, and it becomes, not unfrequently, necessary for the citizen to form his opinion upon them. In historical and political memoirs, letters become equally often subjects of great importance.

The only safe and just rule, for the interpretation and construction of private letters, is, that we discard every thing which is not a bare statement of fact, or carries along with it irresistible evidence of truth. Even the statement of facts ought to be given, so as not to require any completion on the side of the receiver of the letter, and which the letter-writer knew would be added by the person addressed during the perusal. As to every thing else, the language of a private letter is so entirely founded upon the relation between its writer and the receiver, their acquaintance with each other's character, use of words, nay, sometimes with the very accent with which the writer is in the habit of pronouncing certain sentiments or words, and upon a knowledge of so many details, which, though unmentioned, serve to give the right meaning to the words, that a letter, destined to remain private, frequently changes its whole character as soon as it is made public, and a third person attempts to interpret whatever can be doubtful or ambiguous. The relation between two persons forms a key to their correspondence, for which nothing else can be substituted. There is a private *usus loquendi* between friends, husband and wife, members of a family, &c., which cannot be known by others.

May it be repeated once more, for, unfortunately, it is but too important, that we ought to be fairly convinced of the genuineness of the letter in question. We cannot be too careful, in times of great excitement, to act upon this principle; for forged letters will often be given to the public, and though the forger is sure that the forgery must be discovered, he perhaps calculates only upon the next effect, and does not care whether the forgery becomes known at a later period or not.

The rules of epistolary hermeneutics apply still more forcibly to private journals. A journal consists of a series of memoranda addressed to one's self, and it is impossible for any other person to discover the precise meaning of any ambiguous expression. A private journal withdraws itself entirely from the common rules of criticism and interpretation. Sometimes from the very rules of logic, for a thousand different and indiscoverable motives may have prompted the writer to have expressed himself, and not otherwise. The words themselves receive, not unfrequently, a different meaning, which is well understood, because the writer addressed them to himself, but not by others.

These remarks acquire still greater importance, whenever letters and journals are admitted as evidence in legal transactions. Private journals and memoranda, or any writing, if they have never been communicated to any one, are now justly excluded in most countries from the courts of justice. It was not always the case, as is well known, for instance, from the trial of Algernon Sidney. No one, who has not himself undergone trials, founded upon letters, memoranda, and journals, and been called upon to explain doubtful or suspicious passages, can possibly form an idea of the difficulty, not only for any stranger to arrive at their true sense, but for the writer himself to place others in that precise point of view, from which the various pieces of this species of writing can be rightly understood.

The same may be said of any manuscript remarks found in the possession of a person, before they have been communicated to others. Those who are not in the habit of noting down their thoughts, which some occurrences of the day may have suggested, do not know that such ideas may be written down with a positiveness, in which the writer is far from desiring to communicate them to others, or he may have set them down, such as the opponent might use against him, without giving his sanction to the whole, or even to any part of it. As to a legal point of view, that which has never left my desk has never left my breast; remarks, before being communicated to any one, are, though written, legally, but thoughts. Such, at least, is the honest principle which ought to be adopted every where. If they are notes of facts, they may of course serve to bring out the truth, like any thing else, which may serve to shed light on an important point; so far as it goes.

IV. *Speeches.* Speeches can be correctly interpreted or construed, only, if we pay attention to the following points.

1. To all the circumstances under which they were delivered; and, among these again, we ought

to weigh well the general character of the meeting, the capacity of those to whom the speech was addressed, their number, whether they were constituents, fellow representatives, or other citizens, which gives a very different character to a speech ; and in what situation the speaker uttered it.

2. Whether it bears the character of having been prepared before-hand, or of being the sudden effusion of the moment ; whether the utterer charges, or has been charged, provokes, or has been provoked.

3. To the fact that in general, a speaker has to use more impressive and emphatic language than a writer, because he has to attract and rivet attention, while the reader does not take up a book unless he is disposed to direct his attention to the work, and because a reader can weigh at leisure the arguments and position of the author ; the hearer of a speech cannot do this so conveniently ; the word of mouth is fleet.

4. Due deduction is to be made on account of the excitement of the moment.

5. We must seek in the whole life and experience of the speaker, for a key to what he declares in the speech, by way of principle or expediency. Men will sometimes make statements, which, separated from their connexion, may have a very alarming appearance, and yet the whole life of him who uttered

them may convince us, that the meaning of what he said cannot be such as it appears. We are bound, in such cases, to allow due weight to a man's life, and to construe his words accordingly; until facts prove that a change has actually taken place in the sentiments of the individual.

6. We must inquire whether the speech assumes more, or less, the character of special pleading. Burke's and Sheridan's speeches, during the trial of Hastings, would form very doubtful foundations for historical inquiries, without due regard being paid to this rule.

These rules are simple, and, indeed, would not recommend themselves, were they not chiefly founded upon good faith and common sense; yet are they daily disregarded, not only in the heat of party strife, but by the historian. How frequently are speeches quoted for or against a point, which would lose all weight, or, perhaps, have an effect opposite to the intended one, were these simple rules properly attended to. The same applies to historic anecdotes, often repeated for centuries, and yet of no value, if duly criticised.

In regard to the application of the first principle of criticism to speeches, namely: convince yourself of the genuineness of the text, it is necessary to remark, that neither professional reporters, nor, always, our own ears are sufficient guarantees for the genuineness of the text. We may misunderstand the utterer, especially in the noise of public assemblies, and an opportunity of fair explanation should not only be granted, but, if it depends upon us, should be offered.

Remarkable instances of the interpretation or construction of speeches have taken place in legislative assemblies, when they have become the subject of parliamentary inquiry. Mr. Manuel was expelled from the French chamber of deputies, in February, 1823, in consequence of an unfavorable construction put upon an unfinished sentence of his own. Our newspapers, political and religious, furnish but too frequent instances.

That pamphlets, written in times of great excitement, are to be interpreted and construed at the time, as well as by the later historian, with all the care which speeches require, would not be necessary to mention here, were they not so frequently used in a different way.

V. Orders and directions of a passing nature, in the army, navy, executive departments, or wherever they may be given, are not unfrequently penned in a manner, which admits of and demands interpretation and construction. They are always to be understood with reference to the known and general object of the utterer. In drawing them up, the well-known points are omitted; because the text is not to become the general rule of the actions of many or of successive generations as a law. Interpretation and construction must, in these cases, go as far as common sense dictates, at the responsibility and peril of the receiver of the order. The more implicit the order, therefore, is intended to be, the more clearly it ought to be worded, yet its subject, or the time at which it is given, is frequently of a character which excludes any extensive writing. The orders, which Napoleon gave to his chief commanders on the eve of battle, are considered by military men as models of brevity and perspicuity; and yet they make that allowance for free action, which is so indispensable for those, who have to execute charges of the highest responsibility. I have been told that the first order which General Scharnhorst issued, in order to arm all Prussia, in the year 1813, was in so small a compass, that his aids could write it on a small parchment tablet. It is evident that nothing essential could have been done, had not those who received this momentous order construed it in the broadest manner, especially when we consider that this very order was issued at a time, when a fearful enemy was yet in possession

CHAPTER VI.—SECTION VI. 159

of a great part of that country, which was to rise against him within a short time.

It may be adopted as a rule, that the greater a man, placed in high spheres of action, the more distinctly he will give indeed the few essential points, upon which mainly some great action depends, but the less inclined he will also be found to fetter his agents by pedantic minutæ. See Wellington's Dispatches. If so, however, these few great points require proper construction, extensive, comprehensive construction. So do we likewise find the dispatches of great statesmen to agents who are treating of a peace. The main points will be given, the minor are left to proper construction, and it will be always found, that if a plenipotentiary acts under such a minister, against an agent of a pedantic statesman, the former will invariably get the better of him.

VI. *Contracts, Deeds, Wills, &c.* Their construction forms a most important subject of law; but the rules relating to them and to the positive law of every country, ought to be given connectedly, in order to be properly understood. They belong to the proper province of law. Whenever the private citizen has officially to decide upon these subjects, it is the duty of the judge to charge him in a perspicuous manner, according to his capacity. He is often, however, called upon to form an opinion, especially upon contracts, and other deeds; as a private individual, and for this purpose it is desirable, that a jurist of high eminence should draw up a popular work on the construction of contracts, deeds, and wills. A work of this sort would be of great advantage to the community at large.

I must refer the reader for information upon legal instruments, emanating from private individuals, or establishing certain legal relations between them, to 2 Blackstone, 379, and sequel, and the various places where the commentator speaks of wills; and Kent's Comment. II. 552, IV. 344, 345. In the former place (Kent, II. 552) the student will find several other works referred to, especially lord Bacon's *De Augmentis Scientiarum*, by a thoughtful perusal of which, the student will do himself a great service.

Wherever a great mind, or many of the most prominent men of a nation jointly, have endeavored to express the essence of laws after mature reflection, we are bound to their attentive study, because their object has been carefully to separate that which is accidental, or transient, from the essential or enduring. In this respect, it will be always useful to inquire into the codes of those nations, who have codified their various laws, and who acknowledge the same fundamental views of civilization with ourselves. Their codes are not the capricious inventions of the closet, but contain the essential principles, which were scattered in their accumulated laws, anterior to the codification, now embodied into one systematic whole. We need not, indeed, adopt on this account the various provisions of these codes; they may be in some cases repugnant to the principles of our civil institutions; but they will always furnish us with ample matter for fruitful reflection, and not unfrequently lead us to wiser opinions, or strengthen us the more firmly in our own. It goes far to prove the truth of a principle, at which we have arrived, if we find that it has likewise been laid down, after patient deliberation and careful inquiry into the experience of centuries, by a nation disconnected from our own, and grown up under different institutions. In some cases, the evidence even becomes the stronger with the greater difference of the two nations, provided always we can show that the law or principle was not laid down by the foreign nation, for some sinister purpose, or starting from principles entirely at variance with those which we acknowledge in corresponding cases. This, however, belongs more properly to the subject of authorities, and more will be said on it farther below.[1]

VII. *Laws.* It has been shown that it is impossible to word laws in such a manner as to absolutely exclude all doubt, or to allow us to dispense with construction, even if they were worded with absolute (mathematical) distinctness, for the time, for which they were made; because things and re-

---

[1] Prussian Code, Part I. Tit. IV. 65, and *seq.* as to Wills. Part I. Tit. XII. 519, and *seq.* Part I. Tit. V. 252, and *seq.*, and Part II. Tit. VIII. 2109, and *seq.* French Civil Code, 1156, 1164, as to Wills, 967, 1035. Austrian Code, the whole 17th Book of Part II. treats of Contracts; the whole of the 9th Book of Part II. of Wills. The digest under the proper heads, and, with regard to Construction, L. 50, Tit. XVII. *de diversis regulis juris antiqui*, which will amply repay serious and comprehensive reflection, *legant eos (titulos) studiosi juris, ac relegant, meque sponsore credant, nunquam fore, ut eos impensæ operæ pœniteat.* Heineccii *Elementa Juris Civilis*, ed. quinta, tom. II. 350.

The Grounds and Maxims of the English Law, by William Noy, attorney general, in the reign of Charles I., is a book which ought to be mentioned here. The student ought not to remain unacquainted with it, because it has some valuable parts, and continues to maintain a respectable place among the English law books—a fact which will always lend historical interest to it at any future period. Yet there is a great lack of comprehensiveness of mind, and philosophical penetration, in this work. It would be a matter of serious regret, indeed, had science, by this time, not far advanced beyond the sphere of Noy's book, and though law, as well as practical life, have improved and thus mended its deficiencies, it is to be lamented that no work has been produced long ago, able to render Noy comparatively useless. The subsequent editions of this book can by no means be considered as having changed the character of the work. I would, likewise, refer once more to Vattel's chapter on Interpretation; respecting contracts, to Story's Commentaries on the Conflict of Laws, p. 225, 232.

lations change, and because different interests conflict with each other. The very object of general laws is to establish general rules before-hand ; for if we would attempt to settle each case, according to the views, which, with the momentary interest, it might itself suggest, we should establish at once the most insufferable tyranny or anarchy. This inherent generality, however, is likewise the reason, why the application of laws requires construction, since most cases occurring are of a complex character. It is in vain, therefore, to believe in the possibility of forming a code of laws absolutely distinct, like mathematical theories. All that true wisdom requires is to make laws as distinct and perfect as possible, following both the dictates of reason and the suggestions of experience, and carefully to establish rules of interpretation and construction, or legal hermeneutics.

As it has been so often asserted, and to this day continues to be asserted by some persons, that laws ought to be so clear that interpretation or construction can, and, therefore, ought to be abandoned, I feel obliged briefly to enumerate the causes, why this is impossible ; in doing which, I shall be pardoned if I touch upon a few subjects, which have been treated already at length, in order to be the clearer on this very important subject. Yet I also declare my settled conviction, that the clearest possible laws are an incalculable blessing to a community, extending much farther than merely to the avoiding of unnecessary litigation; whilst obscure or unnecessarily intricate laws are a very curse to a nation, and serve to unite the lawyers into a compact, formidable and privileged class, to be compared only to the priesthood of some nations, ruling the uninitiated. I allude to a state of things such as exists in the Spanish colonies, or in the kingdom of Naples, or in some branches of the British law.

There is a law in the Chinese Penal Code, as translated by Sir George Staunton—a work which has many praiseworthy traits—that may fairly be considered as a model of ambiguous laws, to which all others approach, more or less. The Chinese Code says, ' Whoever is guilty of *improper conduct*, and such as is contrary to the *spirit* of the laws, though not a breach of any specific article, shall be punished at the least with forty blows; and when the *impropriety* is of a *serious nature*, with eighty blows.'[1] This is a law clearly emanating from the

---

(1) It may be observed here, that the blows in the Chinese Code, are frequently mentioned as the expression of value, as it were. A fine of so much is substituted for a certain number of blows. They are the pound sterling of penal valuation. However, the compounding ceases with the lowest classes, where real pounding takes place.

spirit which pervades the whole Chinese empire, that the emperor is the father, the whole country but a family—a principle which necessarily always leads to absolutism and tyranny, the moment we go beyond the family, in which affection is the base, and not right; while personal affection cannot form a fundamental principle, where personal connexion ceases, and government acts by delegation, as I have endeavored to show ere this.[1] This ambiguous and dangerous law would be, in its spirit, not as to the blows, a perfectly proper family rule.

Interpretation and construction of laws, then, become, or may become, necessary:

On account of the character of human language, as has been shown.

On account of their ambiguity, either arising from a want of acquaintance with the subject legislated upon, on the part of the legislator, or from contradictions in the law itself.

On account of their application to complex cases.

On account of the change of circumstances and things to which they must be applied, or of the spirit of those by whom they are applied, as was the case with many English penal laws until very late, which the jurors would not, and could not apply without ample construction.

(1) Political Ethics.

On account of their militating, if applied to certain cases, or in certain parts, with more general and binding rules; whether these latter be constitutional, written and solemnly acknowledged rules, or moral ones, written in the heart of every man.

VIII. What has been said respecting all the specific rules applicable to contracts, &c., holds, likewise, in regard to laws. They cannot possibly all be given here; but the most general rules and principles find here a proper place, and that the reader may have an easy survey of them, a few which have been given already as rules, are applicable to all interpretation, are briefly repeated here.

The student is referred, for a further pursuit of this study, to the 12th chapter of the 5th Book of Pufendorf's Law of Nature and Nations, as, likewise, the 17th Title of the 50th Book of the Digest, which we have cited in the previous paragraph. The principles, there laid down by the ancient civilians, as well as the whole code, have materially influenced the common law of England. See Kent's Comment. Lect. XXXIX. 12. See, also, Grotius de Jure Belli et Pacis, Lib. II. Cap. XVI. de Interpretatione.[1]

(1) I would refer, likewise, to the works and places mentioned in the previous section; also, to the article on the Interpretation of Law, in the London Law Magazine, No. 36, &c.

The following are the most general rules:

1. The true meaning of words can be but one.

2. Honest, faithful, *bonâ fide* interpretation is all important; common sense must guide us.

3. Words are to be taken according to their customary, not in their original or classical, signification.

4. The signification of a word, or the meaning of a sentence, when dubious, is to be gathered from the context, or discovered by analogy, or fair induction. Yet the same word does not always mean the same, in the same discourse or text. This would, in fact, militate with the important rule, that we are to take words in their natural sense, according to custom and their connexion.

5. Words are always understood as having regard to the subject-matter.

6. The causes which led to the enactment of a law are guides to us. If one interpretation would lead to absurdity, the other not, we must adopt the latter. So, that interpretation which leads to the more complete effect, which the legislator had in view, is preferable to another.

For the above rules see Blackstone and Pufendorf. As to rule 6, see Dig. L. 50, Tit. 17, 67.

7. Two chief objects of all government are peace and security; the state can never be understood to will any thing immoral, so long as there is

any doubt. Laws cannot, therefore, be construed as meaning any thing against the one or the other. Security and morality are the supreme law of every land, whether this be expressly acknowledged or not.

8. The general and superior prevails over the specific and inferior; no law, therefore, can be construed counter to the fundamental law. If it admits of another construction, this must be adopted.

Lord Coke was for holding laws void that were *contrary to reason.* Chancellor Kent says, Comment. III. 448: 'But while we admit this conclusion of the English law (namely, that the will of the British legislature is the supreme law of the land, and demands perfect obedience,) we cannot but admire the intrepedity and powerful sense of justice which led lord Coke, when chief justice of the K. B., to declare as he did in Doctor Bonham's case, that the common law doth control acts of parliament, and adjudges them void when against common right and reason. The same sense of justice and freedom of opinion, led lord chief justice Hobart, in Day v. Savage, to insist, that an act of parliament made against natural equity, as to make a man judge in his own case, was void; and induced lord chief justice Holt to say, in the case of the city of London v. Wood, that the observation of lord Coke was not

CHAPTER VI.—SECTION VIII. 169

extravagant, but was a very reasonable and true saying. Perhaps what lord Coke said in his reports, on this point, may have been one of the many things that King James alluded to, when he said, that in Coke's Reports there were many dangerous conceits of his own, uttered for law, to the prejudice of the crown, parliament, and subjects.' No doubt, they are dangerous to the pretensions of a king whose arrogance was equalled by his want of judgment, courage, honesty and decency.

Our courts have repeatedly declared laws void as being against the constitution. For the various American cases, confirming this necessary doctrine in all countries, in which there is a constitution, see Kent's Comment. sect. XX., where the commentator speaks in just terms of that beautiful argument delivered on this vital question, by chief justice Marshall, in the celebrated case of Marbury v. Madison (1 Cranch, 137,)—an opinion which is of the utmost importance in the constitutional history of mankind.

9. A law, contrary to the fundamental or primary law, may at any time be declared so, though it has already been acted upon; for 'that which was wrong in the beginning cannot become valid in the course of time.' Dig. L. 50, Tit. 17, 24, and

'Quod ab initio non valet, in tractu temporis non convalescit.'

This does not militate with the other maxim given by Noy that, 'Communis error facit jus.' This is true so long as 'the communis error' is not acknowledged as such, and if we do not understand by *jus* an immutable thing, which, therefore, on proper grounds may be declared to be non-jus. Else, should it have remained forever *jus* to burn witches? Common, assuredly, the error was, for it has been computed, that in the whole nine millions five hundred thousand beings were sacrificed as witches or wizzards, not to mention the countless victims of the most barbarous torments.[1]

10. If, therefore, the law admits of two interpretations, that is to be adopted, which is agreeable to the fundamental or primary law, though the other may have been adopted previously.

11. Custom of the country, where the law was made, supplies the deficiency of words.

12. In dubious cases, the fairer interpretation is to be adopted. 'Every where, especially in law, equity is to be considered.' Dig. L. 50, Tit. 17, 90, 192, 200.

(1) The Revelation of God, &c. by Henry Stephani, DD. 1835, (in German) 1 vol. page 194. Dr. Stephani computes, of course, the number of the victims of witch trials in christian countries only.

CHAPTER VI.—SECTION VIII. 171

13. That which is probable, or customary, is preferable to that which is less so, wherever obscurity exists.

14. If two laws conflict with each other, that must yield, the effect of which is less important; or that is to be adopted, by the adoption of which, we approach nearest to the probable or general intention of the legislator. Specific rules, adopted for the protection of private individuals, must be followed.

Whether the laws were made by the same legislator, or body of legislators, or not, does not alter the case. For the legislative power in a state is continuous, aiming, or supposed to aim, at the public welfare.[1]

15. The more general the character of the law is, the more we ought to try strictly to adhere to the precise expression. Without it, it would be a wavering, instead of a stable rule, and we must presume that the words have been the better weighed. Many considerations, however, may exist, which would oblige us to follow a different course, e. g., the cruelty of a law, its antiquity, and consequent unfitness.

[1] See Puffendorf's instance of two men arriving at the same time at the gaol, or the conflicting laws with regard to a woman who had deserved a statue.

16. If any doubt exists in penal laws, or rules, they ought to be construed in favor of the accused; of course, without injury to any one else.

17. In cases of doubt between the authority and an individual, the benefit of the doubt, all other reasons being equal, ought to be given to the individual, not to the authority; for the state makes the laws, and the authority has the power; yet it is subversive of all good government, peace, and civil morality, if subtlety is allowed to defeat the wise object of the law, or if a morbid partiality for an evil-doer guides the interpreter.

18. The weak (hence the individual arraigned by the state) ought to have the benefit of doubt; doubt ought to be construed in mercy, not in severity; a law may be rendered milder, but not more severe.

IX. *Constitutions.* Constitutions are always laws and guarantees—'sponsio communis'—the fundamental and organic law, and in many cases they are actual and solemn pacts and covenants. In another work I have endeavored to show, that in countries in which the rulers do not directly come from the people, and periodically return to them, but, on the contrary, are as to their appointment removed beyond the influence of the people, in all hereditary governments, but especially in monarchies,

CHAPTER VI.—SECTION IX. 173

constitutions are always in a certain point of view to be considered as contracts between the people on the one side, and the ruling race or dynasty on the other, whether nominally made as contract or granted by the monarch, so long as either party insists on the maintenance of the constitution, and does not allow the other party to break it. The preamble of the instrument does not change the matter, and the French charter granted by Louis XVIII. was a solemn compact so long as either party repelled the aggressions of the other; and when the party of the rulers finally came to invalidate the constitution in some of its vital points, the nation did not reason on the ground that as the king had given it, the king might take it, but that the charter is a solemn covenant, and to subvert it is subverting the very foundation of government, throne and all, and in remodelling the charter we find a declaration 'that the throne is vacant de facto and de jure,' among other things substituted for the previous preamble in which were the words: *Nous*, that is, the king, *avons volontairement et par libre exercice de notre autorité royale accordé et accordons, fait concession et octroi à nos sujets*, &c.[1]

(1) In French, a constitution, nominally or really granted from the mere grace and good will of the ruler, is called *octroyée*. Hardly had I published in the article Constitution, in the Encyclopœdia Americana, the following remarks, when the French

Some constitutions assume more or less the distinct character of a contract, or even that of a treaty, made by contracting powers, such as the constitution of the Germanic confederacy; others are general rules which have been settled and expressed, as much in order to lay down general principles of action, so that disorder may be prevented, and every citizen may know what he may safely do, and what he ought to avoid, as to limit the power of those in authority, that they may not make improper and dangerous use of it. This is the case with the state constitutions in the United States.

revolution of 1830, proved that all France took the same view. A chartered constitution, or '*constitution octroyée,* partakes much of the nature of a compact, as soon as the people have sufficient spirit and sense of justice to prevent it from being infringed or abolished, and, asserting the natural rights of men, whose rulers exist only for their benefit, avow that they will submit to the government only as long as the government observes the constitution. In fact, a constitution *octroyée*, in any case, can hardly be regarded otherwise than as a compact, proceeding, as it does, from the wants of the times and the demands of the people, and expressing the intention of the ruler to observe certain rules, which these wants and demands prescribe. Where would be its value, how could it be regarded as a fundamental law, controlling the operations of the government, if it were liable to be abolished at any moment, at the pleasure of the sovereign? That the monarch acted from compulsion in granting the constitution, only proves that the character of the times made it indispensable. The French ultras are grievously mistaken, when they pretend that the king may abolish the *Charte* because he granted it. It is not the words with which it is prefaced, but the circumstances under which it was given, that are to determine its character. It was granted to satisfy the demands of the French people, and as a pledge for the security of their liberties; and as long as they hold to the grant, it is impossible for the ruler to recall it. Such a constitution, therefore, may be considered as resting virtually on a compact.'

CHAPTER VI.—SECTION IX. 175

If we survey all political constitutions with reference to our subject, we shall find the following classes:

Constitutions, which consist of a declaration of rights, whether freely established by the people, or granted by the authority, or wrung by the former from the latter, and of certain broad principles, which are to be observed in governing the people; but not of a description of the form of government, and a limitation of the various authorities thereof; such as the English declaration of rights, although the law and custom deposited in the long history of England, form a very detailed constitution.

Constitutions, which aim at defining the government and its powers, and are the emanation of the sovereign will of a whole state or nation.

Constitutions, which are formal compacts between a nation and a ruling race. They originate, when a family not fully or clearly entitled to the throne is called to occupy it, on the distinct understanding contained in the constitution; such was the case with Louis Philippe, king of the French, Leopold, king of the Belgians, Bernadotte, king of Sweden, and several others; or they may originate after civil strifes between the people and their rulers, and, in these cases, are laid down as the distinct compact on which, for the future, the two parties are agreed to support and protect each other.

Constitutions, which consist in formal compacts between contracting powers, independent of each other before the conclusion of the compact, where distinct points are granted and limits defined; as was the case with the United Provinces of the Low Countries, and is the case with the United States of America, the cantons of Switzerland, and other confederacies. These latter constitutions will always be more or less affected by a most powerful element, which nevertheless may be, strictly speaking, extra-political, namely, by the principle of nationality. A confederacy may consist of sovereign members, and yet language, religion, common civilization, common origin, in short a common history, may furnish most powerful ties and influential elements besides the pronounced and strictly acknowledged political ties of the union.

X. In considering the construction or interpretation of constitutions, it is necessary to mention, once more, that wherever human language is used, interpretation or construction becomes indispensable, even with regard to constitutions. The constitution of the United States says: that congress shall have the power of regulating commerce, but it does not say how far this regulatory power shall extend. This sentence, then, must be interpreted, if we are

CHAPTER VI.—SECTION X. 177

desirous to ascertain what precise meaning the framers of our constitution attached to it, and construed, if we are desirous of knowing how they would have understood it respecting new relations, which they could not know at the time, and which nevertheless fall decidedly within the province of this provision. The many debates, at various periods, on this very provision, sufficiently prove that it is differently understood by different men and parties, and that consequently, conscientious construction is called for. The question is not, shall we construe at all? but: what are the safe and general rules of political construction?

To argue, as has been done, that the necessity of construction shows the futility of constructions, is altogether inadmissible, for it would equally apply to any law whatever, to all contracts and wills, to any human language, and to the bible no less than to political codes.

The following rules appear to me the most essential in constitutional hermeneutics:

1. A primary rule, suggested by mere common sense, and yet so frequently abandoned, both in religion and politics, and always the more flagrantly so the more men are obliged by the unsoundness of their view, to resort to special pleading is, that we ought not to build arguments of weighty importance

on trifling grounds, not to hang burdens of great weight upon slight pegs; for instance, an argument of the highest national importance upon the casual position of a word. This rule applies to all and every construction, indeed, but it naturally becomes the more important, the more important the sphere is in which we have to construe.

2. If no genuine construction of any text whatever can take place without good faith and conscientiousness, it is most especially the case with regard to politics; for no human wisdom can possibly devise an instrument, that may not be interpreted so as to effect any thing but that for which the constitution was established, or the fundamental principles laid down. We gain nothing by verbosity, or a minute enumeration of details; for a constitution is to embrace all branches, and hold good for many generations. If we attempt, then, to detail every thing before hand, we only impede, fetter, and obstruct. Experience has fully proved this. On the other hand, if the constitution contains only the great principles and general outlines of the state, faithless interpretation has free play. Where, then, is the essential guaranty of liberty? No where, but in the breast of the citizen. Constitutions are useful, and indispensable for the clear understanding of each other on the most important subjects of society, and

a manly knowledge of that all-important element of right and civil liberty — the relation of the individual to the political society in the aggregate — the state, as well as for furnishing to an independent judiciary, a fulcrum to rest its lever on, against laws hostile to that true relation of the individual to the state laws, which otherwise must crush the individual. But constitutions do not make liberty; liberty is not decreed in so many words on parchment. That parchment, with its ink upon it, may be eaten by the worms, may be torn by any daring hand; but if they are but the pronouncing and solemn expression of that which lives within the nation, the written words of the living essence, it is far otherwise.

Under the best constitution, political crimes and offences of all sorts can easily be committed, as soon as the spirit of the people allows those in power to construe it for that purpose; and a people, animated by a manly spirit, may force those in power to construe an unfavorable constitution and dangerous prerogative, agreeably to the civil spirit which animates the whole society. Imagine the English constitution with a lax, yielding, degenerate or servile people — imagine? Look at the history of Henry VIII. What is there that a minister might not do, if he had a mind to betray his nation, and if the people would let him do it, without in one single instance acting against the letter of the law of Great-Britain. As to words, the privileges of the crown are immense. The very efficiency of parliament hangs by very slender threads, as to the words or forms of the constitution; but can a minister discard parliament? The whole history of James I. and his successor is but one continued commentary upon the fact, that faithless interpretation and construction will be able to defeat the true object of almost any form of words.

It is, as was alluded to already, not otherwise in religion. We shall do to others as we wish others to do unto us. Faithless construction might say, I wish to lead a life of licentiousness, and am perfectly willing, nay, desirous, that others should lead it.

Blackstone, in the fourth volume of his Commentaries, in a note to page 439, says, with great naïveté: 'The point of time at which I would choose to fix this *theoretical* perfection of our public law, is the year 1679; after which, the *habeas corpus* act was passed, and that for licensing the press had expired, though the years which immediately followed it were times of great *practical* oppression.' The italicising is not my own; yet the commentator has marked them as if to illustrate the above rule.

The constitution of the Brasilian empire is founded on decidedly liberal principles; but how are the people treated, or rather, what do they make of it themselves? The constitution of the United States bestows prerogatives upon the president, which might deprive the people of all liberty, the moment they should become indifferent enough to allow it. Nor do I say that less power ought to have been conferred upon the American chief magistrate. It would be a great mistake to suppose, that any thing would be gained by merely tying the hand of the executive; then the power would be somewhere else, and equally obnoxious to abuse.

3. The principle, that 'the general prevails over the particular,' is of great importance with regard to constitutions; it amounts to saying, that the 'public welfare is the supremest law of every country, is above the supreme law.' Even the Chinese, 'that nation of incurable conservatives,' acknowledge in their four sacred books, literally the principle, 'salus populi suprema lex.[1]'

There can be no construction, therefore, contrary to this law of laws, or vital principle of every law, all appearance to the contrary. No prerogative, no privilege can exist against public welfare; but in acknowledging this, we must take great care that we do not fall into two serious errors. First, we must

---

(1) Davis's Chinese, London, 1836, vol. 2, the chapters on Confucius, Religion, &c.

have a proper conception of the public welfare, and not understand by this term, as is frequently the case, physical prosperity only, high prices, good wages, flourishing commerce, &c., for though these are concomitant parts of real public welfare, yet they are by no means its only elements, or only tests. They have been, in not a few instances, the dangerous guise, under which absolute power and oppressive tyranny have stolen into the mansion of public liberty. Nothing, indeed, is more common than that usurpers promote industry and commerce. They are generally wise men, who know the great value of national activity, and, apart from their ambitious plans, are frequently men of lofty and noble dispositions, not naturally inclined to harm others, but ready to do so when prompted by their aspiring views. Secondly, we must guard ourselves against mistaking our private views and interests, our passions and appetites, for public wishes or demands; in short, against confounding our individuality with public welfare. This applies to citizens as well as rulers, to each one in his sphere, and naturally so, for all are the same compound beings.

There have been few usurpers, or political transgressors, on a large or small scale, who did not protest, that they have disregarded the law of the land, or the acknowledged principles of civil liberty, because public welfare demanded the violation. It was one of the alleged principles on which Ernest of Hanover lately founded his revolutionary act which annulled the constitution of the land. Yet it remains true on the other hand, that those states are doomed to decline, and fall to ruin, which endeavor to rule by ancient laws and forms only, and obstinately resist the progress and spirit of the age, as if the public mind could be encircled or checked by oral or written sentences.

Those Danes, therefore, were right, who maintained that that most curious of all fundamental laws, by which, in the year 1660, the king was made, by desire of the people, ' hereditary and absolute sovereign,' and, according to which, no fundamental laws should have any force, except the one, that nothing should bind the king — that even this law only had a meaning, by tacitly supposing that the king would use this power for the welfare of the people.

4. Constitutions should be, in ordinary cases, construed closely, because their words have been well weighed, and because they form the great contract or agreement, between the people at large, or between the people and their ruling race. It matters not, as has been stated, whether the constitution declares, that it is a free gift of the sovereign's

bounty, as did the French charter of Louis XVIII; for, on the one hand, as soon as the people accept of it, and as long as they insist on it, it is a *bonâ fide* contract; and on the other, it is well known, that no sovereign grants a charter, except when circumstances require it. The very charter proves it.

5. The more a constitution partakes of the character of a solemn compact, the closer its construction must be; for we have no right to construe or interpret otherwise, if there are several parties. Construction of federal constitutions, therefore, ought to be close; especially if they distinctly pronounce, that the authority and power granted therein is all that is granted, and that nothing shall be considered as granted, except what is mentioned, as is the case with the constitution of the United States of America.

6. All the rules which relate to precedents, demand peculiar attention in the construction of constitutions. For on the one hand, one of the great objects of government is security and peace, which includes stability, by which is not only meant the absence of revolutions, but also the certainty of rights, and legal as well as political relations; on the other hand, an unfortunate concurrence may cause a law to be passed, or the people to acquiesce in it; yet, if every law or measure, adopted on the

ground of strong expediency, were always elevated to a principle, it would frequently thwart some of the most important objects of the constitution itself.

We should follow in this particular the Digest, which declares, as one of the *regulæ juris*, L. 50, Tit. 17, 162, quoted before, that 'That which has been adopted from necessity cannot be applied to similar cases.' See farther below on Precedents.

7. Transcendent construction ought to be resorted to, regretting the necessity which obliges us to make use of it, rather than seeking how we may contrive to justify a transgression of power, or stretch the constitution to obtain it. We ought ever to be mindful, that every transcendent construction may be but the beginning of fearful inroads.

8. As we may interpret a will with greater ease than a contract, and a contract, if it relates to a few, who concede, more comprehensively than a law, so we may construe a law with more freedom (provided no party be injured thereby) than a constitution; for the latter contains the most general rules applying to all. They are calculated, then, for something that is common to every one; and, as there can be but fewer things common to all in a large community, than among a few persons, or between two, it is necessary strictly to adhere to those fewer points,

lest we should enter upon something which is not any longer common to all.

9. Seek for the true spirit, which pervades the whole constitution, and interpret in good faith accordingly, provided this spirit is in favor of public welfare, which is not the case with all constitutions, or the instrument be not irreconcilable with the present time, having been established, for instance, in past ages, and according to a spirit, which has long been supplied by a characteristically different one.

Constitutional history proves that it is of moment, that the speaker of the popular house should not only be eligible by the house, but also be independent of the crown; for a speaker without considerable power, impedes rather than promotes the business; but if this influential person is dependent upon the crown, the liberty and usefulness of the house is greatly injured, as we see in the periods of the Jameses and Charleses. The new French charter, therefore, (article 37) takes the power of confirming the president of the deputies, from the crown, which, according to the charter of 1814, it had. The speaker of the British commons, however, must be confirmed by the crown, as the constitution stands, though, of course, the coronal privilege has not been acted upon for a long time. Suppose a minister should advise the crown to disapprove the choice of a speaker on improper grounds, it would be right for the commons to remonstrate, being guided by a most comprehensive construction of this privilege, namely, that it has not been acted upon for many years, that it is against the present spirit of liberty, that the French have seen fit to abolish it, and that they, the Commons, have not proposed a law, rescinding the coronal privilege, because it is understood to be antiquated, except on very momentous grounds.

It was the misfortune of the French nobility, that a part of them insisted upon their privileges, as established by the ancient law, though many of them were excessively burdensome and galling to the people.

10. But if the constitution itself provides for lawful changes of itself, this necessity exists in a far less degree. Still it exists; the case supposed in the previous paragraph is in point. No constitution has easier remedies provided for than the British, inasmuch as Parliament is, according to constitutional terminology, 'omnipotent,' and a law may at any time change the most essential feature of the realm. Parliament might, if public opinion would allow them, abolish the habeas corpus act forever.

11. If the constitution acknowledges the necessary rights of the citizen, civil liberty is benefitted by

close interpretation as the rule, and comprehensive as the exception only; because the former defines and settles, and thus allows a distinct and traditional knowledge of the civil rights to grow up, and to infuse itself deeply, and in a thousand directions into practical life; so that the body of citizens is animated by civil steadiness and manliness, and a deep-rooted love of justice, which teaches them to esteem each other's rights, because they know them.

But if civil liberty and security themselves have grown up only by continued comprehensive construction of old laws, which, for some reason or other, are not changed, or which it may not even be desirable to change, in favor of civil liberty, this comprehensive construction is most important. In short, let, with a manly nation, every thing that is in favor of power, be closely construed; every thing in favor of the security of the citizen and the protection of the individual, comprehensively, for the simple reason, that power is power, and, therefore, able to take care of itself as well, as tending, by its nature, to increase,[1] while the citizen wants protection. For the same reason ought we always to be ready to construe comprehensively in favor of the independence of the judiciary, and against the

---

[1] Political Ethics, vol. I. on Public Power.

executive, because it is all-important that the judiciary be independent, while it has none of those many influential means of the executive, no pageantry, no honors to bestow, but few salaries to dispense, no army, navy, orders, crosses, titles, lawns, or grants of land at its disposal. It rests on opinion — a mighty power, indeed, if it chooses to act, or is not crushed. Hence it must be shielded.

An attentive observer of the political course of France, during the last half century, has probably nothing to deplore so much, as the habitual unsteady construction put upon her fundamental laws by all parties, so that few debates occur in the chamber on any important subjects, in which recourse is not had to the very first principles of government, which lie beyond the constitution, we would almost say, to political metaphysics. The enormous administrations which preceded the revolution, as far back as that of Louis XIV. had rooted up every civil principle, and prevented any steady growth of civil liberty. Absolute governments, whether brilliant or not, have always this effect. Their nature causes it. If a people trusts to personality, its institutions will be undermined. Louis XIV. was considered with a feeling of national vanity, le grand monarque; he died, and in what condition did he leave France?

The reign of Elizabeth, which cannot be denied to have been glorious, tried some institutions severely, because she was so popular. James came and tried to do the same, or excel his predecessor, without having her superior judgment — a revolution ensued; Athens trusted to Pericles and his personal qualities — great, indeed — and neglected her institutions, and when death deprived them of a Pericles, they must allow themselves to be ruled over by a Cleon, the currier. The reign of Frederic William II. after Frederic the Great, might even be mentioned as not without bearing upon the subject.

Of the construction of those two important privileges — the veto and the pardoning power — conferred by many constitutions upon the chief magistrate, I shall treat in the second volume of the Political Ethics.

XI. One of the most important subjects for interpretation and construction, are international treaties. Their very importance, and the extensiveness of the subject, as well as the fact that it has been treated of in various works, induces me to dismiss it here, after one remark only, namely, that treaties being most essentially founded upon good faith, for there is no superior power to enforce them, they require, likewise, most urgently, the same principle in construeing them. Happily it has been found that it is also the most politic way of proceeding. Honest diplomacy is vastly preferable, even on the mere ground of expediency, to that species in which Louis XIV. was such an unwearied adept.

See Vattel's Law of Nations, chap. XVII; Grotius, Puffendorf; and Wheaton on International Law.

CHAPTER VII.

Precedents.—Definition.—Natural Power of Precedents.—Power of Precedent in England.—Reasons of the Powerful Influence of Precedents.—'Wisdom of our Forefathers.'—Lineal Assent, Contemporary Assent.—Great Force, for Good or Evil, of Precedents in Politics.—Reasons.—Distinction between Legal and Political Precedents.—Precedents of a mixed Character.—Precedents necessary for the Development of Law for Civil Liberty.—They settle the Knowledge of what is Law.—Necessary Qualities of sound Legal Precedents.—Executive Acts are no Precedents, except for subordinate Officers, if not against Law.—Fearful Instance of Executive Precedent in the History of the Star Chamber.—No Man shall take advantage of his own Wrong.—Sound Precedents.—Precedents must be taken with all their Adjuncts.—No Precedent weighs against Law and Right.—Still less against Reason.—Precedents must not increase Public Power.—Precedents must settle, not unsettle.—Precedents may be overruled if necessary. The greatest Lawyers have done so, for instance, Lord Coke.

I. In settling that which is uncertain, in law and politics, and, therefore, in construction likewise, great aid is derived from precedents and authorities. I shall treat first of precedents.

A precedent, from *præcedere* to *precede*, to move before, is a case, having happened previous, yet being analagous to, or, in its characteristic points, the same with another before us. In law and politics, precedents signify, in particular, decisions, proceedings, or a course of proceedings, which may serve for a rule in subsequent cases of a similar nature.

The important question is, have precedents any binding power? Ought they to have any binding power, where the question has not been settled that we are to follow them? And if so, why and under what circumstances? Before these questions can be answered, it is necessary to look into the nature of precedents.

II. Precedents possess a natural power, that is to say, they exercise every where a considerable influence upon the judgment of men, in private as well as public life; it is now and always has been the case, with barbarous tribes as well as civilized nations. If a child is chid for some act or other, it thinks to find some extenuation, if it can assert that another child has done the same. When the ministers of Louis Philip, king of the French, a few years ago, issued an ordinance, respecting the erection of some fortifications around Paris, they cited a similar one, issued as early as under Louis XIV.

The most absolute chiefs of semi-civilized tribes are pleased to find real or pretended rules for their acts, in the examples of their forefathers. Few arguments have a greater weight with all early nations, than the assertion of some old and experienced man, that he remembers the father or grandfather of the chief or king to have acted so or so in a similar case. Hardly any measure of government is recommended by the administration papers in free countries, without pointing to a similar and previous case; and if no argument can be found to make an unpopular measure palatable, or to extenuate some act of the executive, this one of recurring to previous cases, if argument it can be called, is sure to be resorted to. And when the British commons struggle with their king for liberty, nothing gives them so firm and solid a support as when they can stand upon a precedent. On what, indeed, did the commons rest their rights in the beginning of their great struggle with Charles I., except on precedents? So powerful is precedent in that country, foremost in the history of constitutional development, that the absence of precedents in high constitutional questions, is, frequently, of equal weight. When earl Danby, under Charles II., was impeached of high treason, and pleaded the king's pardon in bar of the same, the commons alleged ' that there was no precedent that ever any pardon was granted to any persons impeached by the commons of high treason, or other crimes, depending the impeachment,' and thereupon resolved, 'that the pardon so pleaded was illegal and void, and ought not to be allowed in bar of the impeachment of the commons of England'; but they supported their resolution by the reason, 'that the setting up a pardon in bar of an impeachment, defeats the whole use and effect of impeachments; for should this point be admitted, or stand doubted, it would totally discourage the exhibiting any for the future; whereby the chief institution for the preservation of government would be destroyed.'[1] On the other hand, no claims of the crown were so powerful at the most critical periods for British liberty, as those supported, in truth or pretence only, by precedents.

Whence does this natural and universal influence and authority, ascribed or tacitly yielded to precedents, often salutary, often fearful, arise? From various reasons, as the following may show.

(1) Soon after the revolution of 1688, the commons renewed their just claim, and at length it was enacted, 12 and 13 William and Mary, c. 2. that no pardon under the great seal of England shall be pleadable to an impeachment by the commons in parliament. The American constitutions deprive the magistrate, who is invested with the pardoning privilege for common cases, of the same in several cases touching sentences in consequence of impeachments.

III. By citing a precedent, we at once become followers and cease to be leaders; our responsibility, therefore, seems to be divided, or at any rate is shared by some one else. We no longer appear as innovators; there are at least two, that have done the same thing. In matters of a doubtful point of high importance, especially in constitutional matters, we leave, by a precedent, the high seas of theory, and cast anchor in the solid ground of practical life. We moor in reality, and it requires an additional power to weigh anchors, which, for good or evil, have buried their flukes in substantial ground.

If nothing disapproving has been said or done, when a measure took place, we construe silence into tacit assent, tacit permission. Of many actions, however, we can, according to their nature, know only that they have been done, but not what opposition they have met with. The want of knowledge, too, that they were opposed, makes it appear to us that they received a tacit assent.

We all feel, that if we were never to build upon what has been established and decided, but were to begin in every single case entirely anew, progress in any branch would be impossible.

We honor our parents, and the aged, because the probability of greater experience is in favor of them —a kind of reasoning of especial force in those periods in which nearly the whole store of public experience is traditionally handed down, or has to be gathered by personal experience through a long life—in short, when books have not yet, in a considerable measure, supplanted, if not individual experience, for that they never can, yet knowledge of public matters, individually gathered. And secondly, the prima facie evidence of the expediency of a law is in favor of an old one, for what has lasted so long should be supposed not to be inexpedient. Fortescue, in the seventh chapter of his work, De Laudibus Legg. Angl., has a long argument, that the English laws are the best because the oldest.

As to the first, however, we must guard ourselves against a common error, namely, of extending the belief in that wisdom, which we naturally ascribe to persons older and more experienced than ourselves, and especially to our parents and grandparents, in a progressively higher degree, to their parents and grandparents also, in short, to our forefathers; though their lives, and consequently their opportunity for gathering experience, may have been much shorter than ours has already been. This error is attributable to a confusion of ideas. Old may mean a living old man, who may have more experience than a young one; but it may also apply to past generations, which, if all the other circumstances are the same, cannot possibly have had an equally favorable opportunity for experience with ourselves. We are, indeed, as to experience, the old ones, and the past generations the young ones, provided all the opportunities are the same, or we do not throw away the experience of past ages by neglecting faithfully to study them; for in this case, it is very evident, we become again the 'younger ones.' Tacitus says already: 'Nec statim deterius esse quod diversum est: vitio autem malignitatis humanæ vetera semper in laude, præsentia in fastidio esse.¹' Equally erroneous it is if unexperienced arrogance believes that every idea newly occurred to the individual, is on that account new altogether and excellent, and as if the great problem of each day were to nullify all history up to that day. I shall dwell on this important point of political ethics, in the second volume of the work on that subject, and add here only, that the 'wisdom of the forefathers' may be a sentence of sound sense, or entirely empty. It depends entirely upon the fact, what forefathers we mean, and whether they had a favorable opportunity to know much upon the point in discussion. It frequently happens, that a fundamental law of a country is

---

(1) Dial. xviii. Also, Velleius ii. 92. See also Sir Thomas Browne, Vulgar Errors, Adherence unto Antiquity. The second vol. of Pol. Ethics will contain a more full discussion of this subject.

adopted at a period, when universal enthusiasm renders purity of action more common, than is the case in easy times, when self-devotion is little called for, and selfishness diffuses itself in all classes. Thus it was a great epoch, when the American colonies declared themselves free, and there can be no doubt that there was more self-devotion in that congress at Philadelphia, than will be now found in our easy times in an equally large number of men. Those times were more exciting to virtue, and if we speak of the patriotic signers, there is truth in the expression. Not that they were better organized beings, for the favorite saying of lord Nelson, that there are as good fish left in the sea as have come out of it, is very true, but the combination of circumstances was more favorable.

As to the second point, the antiquity of laws, it altogether depends upon the fact, whether they are good or not. Tonnage and Poundage, the ruin of Charles I. were granted first for the life of the prince to Henry V., as a recompense for recovering his right to France, but under a special proviso that it should not be held as a precedent in the case of future kings: 'But yet,' says Sir Edward Coke, ' all the kings after him have had it for life, so forcible is once a precedent fixed in the crown, add what proviso you will.'[1]

(1) 2d. Inst. p. 61. 4th Inst. p. 32.

An old law, moreover, has left a beaten track, it has all the force of custom and habit, which form, in all spheres of human life, strong reasons to adhere to that which is already established. That which is new is disturbing and distracting. These reasons, natural in themselves, operate sometimes most mischievously.

When Sir S. Romilly proposed to abolish the punishment of death for stealing a pocket handkerchief, the Commons of England consulted Sir J. Sylvester, the recorder, and Mr. S. Knowles, the common-sergeant, as to the proposed improvement. They answered, 'that such an alteration would endanger the whole criminal law.' The common objection to any melioration, by those who disrelish it.

IV. Further reasons of the force of precedents or of that which exists already, are, that in politics and law, that species of assent which might be called lineal assent, in contradistinction to cotemporaneous assent, has a different force, from what it has in history. For the question in politics and law is about the continued action of a principle, and if this has been assented to for generations, we must believe there is good ground for it, and leave it untouched, unless we see sufficient and clear reason why we should set it aside; for instance, because times have changed, or assent was not free and voluntary. In history, it disposes us in favor of a statement, if it is proved that its truth was universally admitted at the time. I say it inclines us favorably, but it affords, by no means, sufficient proof, as history or even the affairs of common life frequently prove. Many high personages who died suddenly, have been universally supposed at the time, to have been poisoned. But the lineal assent is of itself of no value whatever in history. If a statement be originally made in such a way, that it excites our suspicion, or is deprived of the force of substantial proof, it becomes no more probable, by the most implicit belief of ever so many centuries. If it can be proved, that some statement with regard to the foundation of Rome, is highly improbable, or involves an impossibility, it matters not whether Livy believed it or not, or whether the middle ages believed Livy, or whether it has been repeated by many thousand authors relying upon Livy or those who subsequently believed him. The number of assenters is of some value with regard to contemporaries, but of none whatever in successive generations, unless the original statement has been subjected to continually renewed criticism. In this case, the degree of our assent is regulated by the keenness and sincerity of subsequent criticism, and not by the fact that many successive generations have, or have not, believed in the first statement. Another instance is the belief in *one* Homer. If it is proved that the poems heretofore ascribed to Homer cannot have been produced by one poet, but must be a collection of poems by various authors, all the belief of the many generations in one Homer has no weight.

But with a nation, with whom liberty has been a practical question for centuries, and with whom it has been long acknowledged that the stability of the law is one of the main ingredients of civil liberty— a nation, moreover,—who did not receive the substance of civil liberty from some other country, but developed it gradually itself, as the English have done, the precedent must acquire a peculiar force. British civil liberty is so powerful a thing, because each important question has come before the commons as a practical case. Law, it was acknowledged by all, should decide, but what was law? The people had nothing but the precedent to protect themselves against encroachment, and though precedents worked fearfully, in many cases, for the crown, yet I believe no historian will hesitate to acknowledge that one of the most essential elements of Anglican liberty, is Precedent. The very fact that something—no matter what—beyond the reach of power was acknowledged as law between the power and the people, was a great principle, not to speak of the immense power which a citizen, struggling for a good cause, has when he can stand upon precedent opposite to power. The whole air of revolutionary innovation, of rebellious resistance, is taken from his act, and the attempt at revolution is thrown on the other party. The king and his servants, therefore, judged correctly when they resolved upon the arrest of Sir Robert Cotton, the antiquarian, because he furnished the leaders of the popular party with precedents.[1] They knew how irresistible a power was latent in those dusty papers; how mighty history is with a constitutional people which has worked for its liberty.

Precedents, like every other thing, may be sadly misapplied. The most absurd as well as the most criminal political acts, are propped with precedents. The corrected calender of pope Gregory XIII. was opposed among other reasons, because to correct or change it was claimed as an imperial privilege, *because* Cæsar had first put it in order, and Constantine ordered the calculation of the feast of Easter to be made at Nicæa! And the history or special

---

(1) Brodie II. p. 155.

law of cities and communities, shows that most of the strangest and exorbitant privileges claimed by individuals or communities over others, are founded upon nothing else but precedents, that is, mere facts. A nobleman extorts from a community so many bushels of grain in one year, *therefore*, he has a right to demand it the next.

It is very necessary, then, that we should ascertain what precedents have binding power, and how far they have it.

V. Before we proceed, however, it is necessary that we should make a clear distinction between legal and political precedents, the want of which has led, at times, to very erroneous and dangerous notions.

A precedent in law, or, as it is called, a legal precedent, is a decision arrived at after patient inquiry into all points bearing upon the doubtful subject, by an impartial judge, who stands between or above the two parties, and is removed beyond the circle of interests within which the two litigating parties move. A legal precedent, therefore, is the settling of a doubtful point by that very authority, which is created by society, among other things, for the settling of doubts between different parties. Society has no better way of making clear and stable that which was doubtful and unsettled. It is evident, that as long as there is no positive reason why we should deviate from such a legal decision, we should adhere to it. Nor is it in any way desirable, that in all matters of legal doubt the highest legislative authority should be appealed to, as is the case in many European states. This leads to a continued and injurious intermeddling of the executive with the law, fetters the independence of the judiciary (one of the very elementary requisites for all liberty,) and throws an impediment in the way of a free and wholesome development of the law, according to the spirit of the nation. Nor is it possible for high authorities to establish general rules, which will apply so precisely to the endless variety of combinations in law, as the authority of precedents is able to do, if rationally limited, and not carried to an idolatry of the past or the established.

As the opposite to legal precedents, we may consider measures of the executive. They differ in their very character from the former. They are not the decision made between two parties by a third and impartial one, but they are nothing but acts. They may be good or bad; they, like any other acts, cannot become better by repetition, if they are bad in the beginning.

Lastly, precedents may be of a somewhat mixed character; they may neither have legal impartiality, nor, on the other hand, be mere acts. Many legislative acts are examples of this kind. Inasmuch as measures are debated, before a legislative assembly adopts them, we may compare them to the balancing of the opposite interests in court; but inasmuch as the legislative assembly does not judge of an occurring case, according to prescribed laws, but, on the contrary, is making these very laws, and inasmuch, also, as the different interests are represented in an assembly of this kind, by two different parties, indeed, but very frequently not impartially weighed by the same persons, their decisions partake of the character of measures and acts, such as we have mentioned already.

VI. We have already seen, that no human wisdom can contrive to make laws, which will precisely cover all complex cases that may occur, whatever attention may be paid by the law-makers to the variety of compound cases, which they are able to imagine; and that it is not in the power of any human intellect, though of the most gigantic grasp, to draw up a political constitution, so as to leave no doubtful case untouched, considering the condition of society at the time of its being drawn up. As to future generations, the problem becomes still more impracticable; because the state of human society is continually changing, and ought to change, according to its very principles of existence. This is a rule, so well established, that statesmen and lawyers are now agreed upon the wisdom of pointing out principles and drawing general outlines in a clear and easily understood language, in constitutions and laws, rather than of giving minute details, which, in whatever degree we may augment the enumeration of minutiæ, have a tendency rather to contract than to extend. It is far easier to act upon laws, in a manner corresponding to the intention of the legislator, when they are brief and clear, and rely upon common sense, than when the details embarrass every step, and prevent the application of the general principle, because the specific case has not been enumerated and singled out by the law-maker.

As it is, however, a well-known maxim in politics and jurisprudence, that the certainty of law is next in importance to its justice — and by certainty of law we understand both that it be well defined, known and unwavering, as also that its penalties fall with unerring certainty upon those who deserve them — it becomes necessary that doubtful points, springing up from a new state of things, should, if once settled, be considered so, until a weighty reason induces us to deviate from the settled decision.

VII. Without this rule, civil liberty, which depends in so high a degree upon a universally diffused knowledge of rights and obligations, as well as upon the stability of government (for instability of government engenders civil immorality), becomes impossible. A citizen, conscientiously desirous of doing right, can obtain no advice from the counsel, whose profession consists in the knowledge of the laws, in any complicated case, if the lawyer himself does not know a certain general rule, or law, which may be applied to the compound case under consideration. Hence, too, we find that the citizens of those countries, in which public liberty has been highly praised, require their rulers to swear, before they assume the highest power, that they will govern according to law and custom; and custom is but precedent. Some of the gravest charges against impeached ministers, or of revolted subjects against their monarchs, have been, that the accused individuals had disregarded the customs of the land.

Without due regard for precedents, no development and expansion of any fundamental law, that is, no expanded application of the principles it contains, commensurate with the expansion of society, and the change and progress of all relations, can possibly take place. If nothing becomes settled, disorder must be the consequence. Words may mean very

CHAPTER VII.—SECTION VIII. 209

indefinite things; it is by practice only, that they acquire definite significations. Is not this the case between friends, or men brought together in any collegiate relation? It is still more the case, in the great political intercourse of citizens.

'The King willeth that right be done, according to the laws and customs of the realme,' &c. The King's Answer to the Petition of Rights, Rushworth, T. 1, p. 590. The king of Great Britain swears, at his coronation, to govern 'according to the statutes in parliament, agreed on, and the laws and customs of the same.'

VIII. In a free country, then, where a knowledge of the citizen's rights is all important, a precedent in law, if correctly and clearly stated — this is an essential requisite — and if applied with discernment, and with the final object of all law before our eyes, ought to have its full weight. If there has been a series of uniform decisions on the same point, they ought to have the force of law, because in this case they have become conclusive evidence of the law. (See Dupin's *Jurisprudence des Arrêts*).

In politics, we ought to follow precedents, which touch upon matters of law, or which partake decidedly of the character of legal decisions upon previously doubtful points, as long as we have no decided and obvious reasons why we should deviate. As, however, most important questions in politics touch upon those broad and original principles, upon which the protection of the citizen, and the security of the state, mainly depend; it will be found, that precedents in this sphere will have far less authority than in law. It is the essential duty of a lawgiver and statesman, to act always on distinct political principles and reasons, and to recur to them in every single case. A deviation from these principles involves a world of injury.

It seems that an imperfection of law, loses, in numerous cases, much of its evil character, merely by the fact of its being universally known; as a piece of rock, which has fallen into a road, is certainly an inconvenience, but if all the people, who are in the habit of travelling that road, know that this obstruction is in their way, they will avoid it, and a travelled road will form itself around it. Its inconvenience is greatly lessened by its being stationary and known; if, however, that piece of rock were frequently moved to different places, the injury to every traveller would be incalculable. Blasting the rock into atoms would be the best course; but, perhaps, it cannot be conveniently done, without injury to the interests of others, or, at any rate, those who travel the road, may not have the means or the right of doing it.

This applies to law; in politics proper, as we have said already, fundamental principles, and a constant recurrence to them, are far more important, on account of the greater importance of these principles.

Whenever we are doubtful, and there are many such cases in law, we should adhere to precedents, because they carry along with them the additional reason of security. The statesman, however, must take into consideration the effects which his measures will have; his decisions will be generally known by their very character; and the greater part of the decisions, at which he will arrive, are rules themselves, and not decisions according to given rules.

IX. Executive acts ought never to be considered as precedents by any one but the inferior executive officer, and he, too, must be conscientiously convinced, that the first act was not against the law. If we were to take every executive act as a precedent, and a justification of similar subsequent ones, it would be monstrous, and subversive of the very principles of a free government. The legal precedent is a decision between parties, but, in this case, the executive itself forms a party. The only point, which might be insisted upon with an appearance of plausibility, would be, that a general acquiescence in a measure, changes it into a precedent; but this is the more dangerous and fallacious, as the act in question is frequently of a kind, that either it cannot be well ascertained, whether general acquiescence has taken place, or that the demonstration of the contrary is impossible. A theory of this dangerous sort would be founded, moreover, upon a principle contrary to free government on another ground. It is one of the fundamental principles of a free government, that a citizen has not only the right of dissenting from those in power, but also publicly to pronounce it, and to unite with others, in order to dislodge by combined strength, and by using fair and honest means, those who are invested for the time, with the insignia of authority. What sense would otherwise the words minority and majority have? It is a most sacred right of every freeman, who belongs to the minority, to convince his fellow citizens, if he can, of the justice of his cause, and gradually to make the minority to which he belongs, the majority. What, however, can the majority do, but to follow the footsteps of the preceding one, if political precedents shall have the authority of legal ones, or any binding power approaching to them. The judge ought not to decide upon his principles, or upon any principles other than those of the established law; the politician stands upon an entirely

CHAPTER VII.—SECTION X. 213

different ground. It is upon the very difference of principles, that a different administration comes into power.

If the legal rules of precedents were to be applied to the acts of the executive, or of any authority which exercises power (for this seems to be the criterion), then any successful transgression of power would at once establish the right of transgressing it for ever. Is there a free country on earth, whose history does not mention repeated instances, when those invested with power or prerogatives, have disregarded some of the rights and franchises of the people, considered by them as vitally important to their liberty and well-being? There is hardly a tyrant ever so vile, who will not, or, indeed, who cannot, cite precedents for his most atrocious offences.

X. As precedents in law are taken from that same law, we can judge better of their value, and whether their authority ought to be perpetuated; but in politics, to take precedents from the history of other nations, becomes in the same degree delusive and dangerous, as that history is less known to us, in all the many details, which may have had a bearing upon the precedent. A rule, that never ought to be departed from, is, that wherever power is supposed to have been unduly exercised, let the case be decided on its own merits; because, as we have seen in a previous chapter, it is the natural, inherent and necessary attribute of all power, physical or moral, that it tends to increase. Moral power is not necessarily evil disposed on this account, but it cannot be power without this tendency; if, then, political precedents should always be entitled to respect, they would only increase and propel, and, therefore, extend, instead of regulating, its motion and effect.

'And that your Majestie would also vouchsafe to declare, that the awardes, doeings, and proceedings, to the prejudice of your People, in any of the premisses, shall not be drawn hereafter into consequence or example.' Petition of rights (drawn up by Lord Coke, then Sir Edward) presented to Charles I. June 2, 1628.

XI. For the same reason, precedents, in regard to questions of doubted jurisdiction, assumed and decided upon by the same court, whose power is doubted, are of less value than those which occur in the decision of law cases. The court here forms a party, and the *stare decisis* does not apply with equal force, as in a proper law decision.

The force of precedents in law, rests partly on

CHAPTER VII.—SECTION XII. 215

this, that similar cases have been decided one way or the other, by men living at a different time or at different places, and when the points in question were argued by different counsel. In this, too, legal precedents differ materially from mandates of the executive construed into precedents.

It may be adopted as a sound maxim, I believe, that the more the advocates of a political measure feel themselves obliged to rely on precedents, the less they ought to be trusted, and on no account ought precedents alone to decide any thing in politics, if doubts exist at all.

XII. Perhaps no case shows more clearly, the danger of taking executive measures for precedents, than the history of the star-chamber. I copy the following from Brodie:

'When this pernicious court was first established by Wolsey, it proceeded with great caution. *The president of the king's council* was added by stat. 21 Henry VIII. c. 20, to the number of judges — a clear proof that, even at this late period, it was conceived to be quite distinct from the council — and by certain acts of Parliament, both in that reign, and even in Elizabeth's, some particular kinds of cases were committed to its jurisdiction. But it, in no long time, assumed a bolder tone, till it even disowned its origin. The whole privy council arrogated the right of sitting there in judgment, and the question was no longer what the statutes allowed, but what the council in former times had done. Having once adopted the principle of precedent, it no longer submitted to any check upon its proceedings. Every act of the council in the worst times, was raked up, though so many statutes were devised against such proceedings; cases were grossly misrepresented; strained analogies were resorted to; and where no shadow of a precedent could be discovered, ingenuity could invent — a proceeding the more simple, as no regular record was kept; while every abominable recent case was held to be conclusive in all future ones. Where no precedent could be discovered or invented, then the paramount, uncontrollable power of a court, in which the monarch might preside in person as sole judge, (for having held it to be the same as the council, they next assumed that principle) was entitled to provide a remedy for any alleged disorder. The judges of this court, too, neglected no means for advancing so arbitrary an institution. Under the pretext of desiring to be directed by the best legal advice, they usurped the power of nominating the counsel who should plead before them; a practice that operated to the exclusion of every man who had honesty and independence

CHAPTER VII.—SECTION XIII. 217

enough to assert the rights of his client. The great Plowden fell under their severe animadversion, for reminding them of stat. 3 Henry VIII. and Sergeant Richardson, about thirty years afterwards, incurred a censure for a demurrer to the same effect. The consequences may, therefore, be easily figured: every precedent begat a worse; and, towards the close of Elizabeth's reign, though the star-chamber still retained some decency, it had reached a monstrous height; but under the Stuarts, it threatened a general overthrow of popular rights, and the engrossment of all ordinary jurisdiction.' Brodie, vol. I. p. 188.

' No man shall take advantage of his own wrong,' is a principle no where of greater importance, than in government precedents.

XIII. Whether we attribute authority to precedents or not, we ought always to pay proper attention to them; for whatever subject may occupy our reflection, it will always be found of great assistance, to inquire how others, in different situations, have viewed and acted upon the matter. New ideas will be suggested, and the subject will appear in different connexions. Mr. Gerard Hamilton (Single Speech Hamilton) gives it as an important rule, in his Parliamentary Tactics, which will be allowed on all hands, to be a work of exceeding shrewdness, whatever we may think of its principles, that whenever a subject previously acted upon, is before the house, we ought to read some works or pamphlets, written at the time when it previously occupied the attention of politicians. Whether we ought first to reflect minutely upon the subject, and then consider precedents, or *vice versa*, must depend upon the conviction we have of our own independence of thought upon the subject. If we know that we are master of the subject, and that our views, upon those principles, which we acknowledge as the fundamental ones of our whole political course, are clear, then we ought first to view the matter in the light of our simple resources alone.

The interests of the moment, the magnitude, with which subjects, in the very midst of which we live, appear, are apt to represent them in too glaring a light, to the injury of other more distant interests. Montesquieu probably meant this, when he said: 'It is with a trembling hand that we ought to change laws.' For this reason, too, precedents demand attention.

XIV. A precedent ought to be sound, that is, it ought to come from good authority, or a period which we consider favorable to a thorough and

CHAPTER VII.—SECTION XIV. 219

sound view of the subject in question. Even James I. said, 'precedents in times of minors, of tyrants, of women, (which was a very unfortunate slip for a James, who followed an Elizabeth) simple kings, are not to be credited, because for private ends.'[1]

Precedents must be taken with all their adjuncts, or they will be totally misunderstood; and not only with their adjuncts at the time, but likewise with their consequences and effects.

No precedent of whatever sort, can weigh against right and distinct law, for the latter are certainty, and precedents are used to obtain approximate certainty in cases of doubt.

Precedents must not increase power against those who are to be protected; for the latter cannot, frequently, oppose the first step of arrogation.

Precedents against law or reason must be set aside. Lord Coke says: 'Quæ contra rationem juris introducta sunt, non debent trahi in consequentiam.'[2]

If the subject which they relate to, has changed, or if we are convinced after patient inquiry, which includes a thorough knowledge of the subject-matter, that we ought in justice to deviate from former de-

(1) Brodie I, 346.

(2) The case of Proclamations, Mich. viii. James I. A. D. 1610. 12 Coke's Reports 74.)

cisions, we act wrong in perpetuating that which is unjust or injurious; for whatever may be said, reason is and must remain above law and precedent. A frivolous or hasty application of this principle is highly dangerous; yet it does not become on this account, the less true. If we should consider all future cases of a similar nature, as prejudged by our decision, stagnation would be the consequence, instead of an expansion and development of the law. There is such a thing as idolatry of precedents, and an idolatry it is, which has slaughtered, at times, Justice at her own altars.

One of the reasons why due weight should be given to precedents, is, as we have seen, the safety and security of the citizens, the steadiness of the knowledge of the law. Adherence to precedents, however, may be carried to such an extent, that its effect is to the contrary. If not only known and acknowledged precedents are followed, but, on the contrary, if that, which according to common sense and justice, ought to be done, is omitted for fear that some hidden precedent to the contrary might exist, then precedents unsettle instead of settling. An effect not unsimilar takes place when something is omitted, which ought to be done, merely because no precedent is known. Surely the first act can have had no precedent; and a precedent unknown in practice, and merely hunted up in the archives, loses its very character of an authoritative precedent.

If the London Evening Mail of April 18, 1834, reports correctly, Mr. Justice Taunton said, in the case of the king on the prosecution of William Seymour, Esq. v. Holloway, 'that, however hard the case might be, (another justice had already declared the case exceeding hard) he did not remember any precedent, which could authorize the interference of the court. The clerk of the court, however, would search among the crown records for a precedent, if such existed, and would inform the learned counsel of it; if there was such a precedent, the learned counsel could bring the matter before the court.'

A precedent in itself, merely as a thing that has happened, or been done, can have no power one way or the other; and the rule, that that which is wrong in the beginning cannot become right in the course of time, is surely too deeply engraven in every man's mind to be doubted. Many of the most eminent lawyers, and we would say, all the most philosophical among them, such as Lord Mansfield, have acted upon this principle, and overruled what was wrong, though with great caution.[1]

---

(1) See the sound and clear exposition of the delicate subject of legal precedents in 3 Kent's Comment. Lect. XXI. p. 479 and seq.

The Roman Law acknowledges the authority of precedents in a far less degree than the English; in fact, if we take the

Thus, the monstrous patent granted by Edward IV. to his father-in-law, Earl Rivers, in the 7th of his reign, giving the vastest powers to the High Constable and Marshall, is explainable only on the ground of the then convulsed state of the country, and necessarily under a sort of military government. Sir Edward Coke, therefore, pronounced it 'a most irregular precedent,' and says that 'therefore by no means the same, or the like, is to be drawn into example. 4 Inst. p. 127. And Lord Bacon, no friend of Coke's, praises Lord Coke's Reports as containing 'infinite good decisions and rulings over of cases.'

word precedent in the English sense, the former does not acknowledge precedents at all, but makes habitual recourse to the emperor, in his legislative capacity, necessary. Those nations, which have adopted the civil law as the main foundation of their own, act upon similar principles. With them, the necessity of judiciary independence upon the executive, is not so clearly acknowledged, as with the Anglican race. It has been shown already that this independence requires, in a considerable degree, the acknowledgment of precedental authority.

The Code, Book I. Tit. 16, 22, declares: 'Si imperialis majestas causam cognitionaliter examinaverit, et partibus cominus constitutis sententiam dixerit: omnes omnino judices qui sub nostro imperio sunt, sciant hanc esse legem, non solum illi causæ, pro qua producta est, sed et omnibus similibus.'

CHAPTER VIII.

Authorities.—Akin to Precedents.—Definition.—Ought we to submit to them?—Slavish Submission to them; Arrant Disregard of them.—We must always adopt Authorities in many Branches.—Main Questions of Historic Criticism.—Similar ones regarding Authorities.—Who is he?—What opportunity had he to know the Subject?--What Motive prompted him? What internal Evidence is there?—Of what Extent is the Authority?—Various Phases of the same Authority.--Classical Periods.

I. The last subject, connected with hermeneutics, which we shall consider, are authorities. We have, of course, not to consider here those authorities which by law we are bound to follow, but only those which we feel morally obliged to acknowledge to a greater or less degree. Many remarks which were made in regard to precedents, apply with equal force to authorities, as most of the observations which will be made on the present subject, hold good in regard to the former, as is necessary from their nature.

II. By authority we understand, in the limited sense in which it is taken here, an individual whose opinion, for some good reason, is of great weight, which, therefore, we use to support our argument, or adopt in doubtful cases, as a rule of action, or whom we follow in cases in which we have not the proper means to inquire into the whole truth, or to arrive at a satisfactory decision by our own judgment alone.

III. The first question here, which we must address to ourselves, is: ought we to submit to authorities at all? Has not every one received an intellect, with reasoning powers to judge for himself? Is it not enslaving the mind to submit it to the opinion of another? These are questions which I do not invent, while writing these lines, but which have been started from time to time, and are at this moment repeatedly asked, and frequently, as I conceive it, answered in a very unsatisfactory manner. There is such a thing as Chinese submission to ancient authority without criticism and reason, and there is such thing as arrant sanculottism disregarding all authority, and leading to licentiousness in morals and religion, not less than in science, law and politics. It is the object of these lines to aid, if possible, in obtaining a clearer view of this subject, which touches the dearest interests of society and the welfare of the individual, and in establishing some rules which may guide us.

IV. 'Implicit faith belongs to fools,' is the title of the first chapter, section three, of Algernon Sidney's Discourses concerning Government, and it might be added: blind obedience belongs to rogues and not to honest men. We must have reasons, why we ought to believe or obey, why we ought to adopt the opinions of others, why we ought to yield to their judgment.

The reason why we ought to yield to the judgment of others is simply this, that each individual cannot be experienced and thoroughly versed in all things, nor has each one possessed the same opportunity to observe, or received the same faculties and endowments for observing all things. If my watch is out of order, my house out of repair, my body out of health, I yield to the opinion of that watchmaker, carpenter or physician, whom for some good reason I consider competent to decide the respective cases. If I write a book on human society, and am desirous to know first of all the physical difference between man and other animals, or ascertain the difference between ancient and modern finances, I inquire what naturalists like Cuvier have said on the former, or scholars like Bökh on the economy of Athens. If I desire to obtain a thorough view of oratory, I see what Cicero has said, or Demosthenes or Fox, Grattan or Pitt, have done in this sphere; the first, because I know that he had a good opportunity to observe and inquire, the latter, because I know they have effected much by their speeches. If a house of legislature are obliged to determine on a subject on which no member has a thorough knowledge, witnesses are examined at the bar or before committees, or the whole subject is first inquired into by a committee, to the report of which the legislature grant that degree of assent, which the peculiar circumstances of the whole case may warrant. A Shakspeare is good authority in many matters of poetry, but not in all. We see, then, clearly two things : we are daily and hourly obliged to acknowledge authorities, but we must have good reasons not only for our acknowledgment, but also for the degree of our assent. No more is demanded in matters of law and politics, than what every one experiences daily in his individual life. We omit a most important duty, if we neglect collecting experience in our life, by impressing the result of important, perhaps dearly paid transactions or events distinctly upon our mind, so that we regulate our actions by them, even at periods, when the details have vanished from our memory, and we only remember that at the time we made up our mind after ample experience, and the result at which we arrived. This applies to cases of expediency, as well as to strictly moral cases. Far greater is the duty of societies in the aggregate, of communities and states to store up experience, for, it cannot be too often repeated, politics are not matter of invention, but of experience; not an abstract science, but the application of the eternal principles of justice and truth to ever varying circumstances.

V. If we are desirous of ascertaining what degree of belief we ought to grant to a historical account, we ought to ask ourselves before all, the following questions respecting the author and the account itself.

Who is he? We ought to know, if possible, where he lived, how he lived, what his connexions, his mental capacity, his morality, his temper, whether rash or cautious, or over-cautious, a matter of fact man, or of ardor and impulse, whether he or his family have suffered, &c.

What opportunity had he to observe? Did he see things, or receive them from the first source, or second hand, or by distant hearsay? Was he engaged in the transactions which he relates; did he take pains to learn the truth?

What motive had he to give this account? Does he endeavor to defend a party, a certain transaction or individual? Could he gain by it, or did he expose himself by giving it? Is he in any manner interested in the matter? Were the times he lived in so agitated by a certain principle, that even unconscious to him is gave a strong bias to his mind, one way or the other, even in viewing events long passed by?

What internal evidence of truth do we find in the account, and how far do those statements which we have in our power to compare with authenticated statements, agree? We possess, not unfrequently, accounts of much importance, the author of which is even unknown to us, and yet they bear such evidence of truth within them, that we cannot otherwise but grant a high degree of faith to them. Instances are found in Raumer's late work containing the correspondence of ambassadors and other persons in high stations, discovered by him in various European archives.

VI. Now, these rules of fair criticism, modified according to the different subjects, are applicable, likewise, to authorities in politics and law. If an authority is cited to which we are expected to grant assent or respect, we ought to ask ourselves first of all:

CHAPTER VIII.—SECTION VII.

Who is he?
What opportunity had he to know the subject?
In what time did he live?
What motive prompted him?
What internal evidence has the authority? and
Of what extent is the authority?

VII. *Who is he?* It is evident, that the whole character of him who is claimed as having established the authority, is of the greatest importance—his moral, mental and political character. That which is applicable to individuals, is no less so as to whole bodies and periods. We must be sure that their character be sound.

Mr. Greenleaf, in an intereresting paper,[1] says:— 'Neither are all reporters entitled to equal consideration; but in weighing the credit which they deserve, regard must be had to their opportunities for observation of what passed in the court, their ability to discern, and their habitual care and exactness in relating. We may listen, with almost implicit deference, to Plowden, and Coke, and Foster; while the authority of some others is entitled to little more respect than was shown to the honest, but blundering Barnardiston, whose cotemporaries, 'who knew the sergeant and his manner of taking notes,'

(1) Professor of Law in Cambridge University, Massachusetts, Introductory Lecture, &c., in the Law Reporter, Boston, Mass., December, 1838.

were surprised rather that he ever stumbled on what was right, than that he reported so many cases wrong. The manner of the decision, too, and the reasons on which it is professedly founded, and even the decision itself, may receive some coloring and impress, from the position of the judges, their political principles, their habits of life, their physical temperament, their intellectual, moral and religious character. Not that the decision will depend on these; but only that they are considerations not to be wholly disregarded in perusing and weighing the judgment delivered. Thus we should hardly expect to find any gratuitous presumption in favor of innocence, or any leanings *in mitiori censu,* in the blood thirsty and infamous Jeffries; nor could we, while reading and considering their legal opinions, forget either the low breeding and meanness of Saunders, the ardent temperament of Buller, the dissolute habits, ferocity and profaneness of Thurlow; or the intellectual greatness and integrity of Hobart, the sublimated piety and enlightened conscience of Hale, the originality and genius of Holt, the elegant manners and varied learning of Mansfield, or the conservative principles, the lofty tone of morals, and vast comprehension of Marshall.

'Neither should we expect a decision leaning in favor of the liberty of the subject, from the Star Chamber; nor against the King's prerogative, among the judges in the reigns of the Tudors, or of James the first; nor should we, on this side of the water, resort to the decisions in Westminster Hall, to learn the true extent of the Admiralty jurisdiction, which the English Common Law Courts have been always disposed to curtail, and in many points to deny; while it is so clearly expounded in the masterly judgments of Lord Stowell, and of his no less distinguished and yet living American cotemporary.'

VIII. *What opportunity had he to know the subject? In what time did he live?* In cases of law, for instance, it is of great importance to know whether the case was amply and thoroughly argued, and whether the opinion now claimed, was given after full investigation, and a detailed examination, or, perhaps, incidentally.

In important political matters, it is necessary to know whether the authority belongs to what we will call a classical age, by which I mean, that period, which by the concurrence of many rare and favorable circumstances, rendered those who lived in it peculiarly fit to see the whole bearing of a question, and which in its result, shows that these questions were thoroughly understood, perhaps sealed with the sacrifice of the dearest interests, even life—periods which, for these reasons, carry a power of victory within them for all successive ages.

A thousand political and religious circumstances, conditions of life and peculiarities of character, cooperated to develope the most exquisite taste in the Grecian tribes. Their sculpture, their architecture, has remained unrivalled, and we are not only permitted, but bound to admit them as good authorities in these branches, if we believe at all in progressive civilization, and that history assigns the development of certain problems to various nations, so that their activity is directed to that point, and that they produce some grand effects, which may benefit other nations without obliging them to go through the same trials, to make the same sacrifices.

We find the same in politics. The very spirit of liberty demands, in all common cases, compromise; a law shall be so poised that it injures the least and benefits the most. The rights of all shall be proportionately honored. An absolute government need not weigh matters with the same nicety respecting existing rights; it disregards them if it has vast plans in view, which ultimately result, or are believed to do so, in a general benefit. If this circumstance is seized upon by enlightened absolute governments, great plans may be carried with comparative ease. Masses may be obliged to yield and work toward the vast object. We have an instance in the Prussian general school system. This being the case, other nations would neglect their duty not to adopt, from this system, those beneficial results which are applicable to their peculiar cases, and offered, without the necessity of adopting the same original means to arrive at them. Polytheism, representing the gods in human shape, which thus came to be idealized, greatly aided in raising the plastic arts in Greece to that eminent pitch of excellence, in which we behold when walking through the Vatican. Let us, at present, reap the fruits, without passing through the same religious mazes. Absolutism aided greatly in effecting that general plan of education, which we behold in its vast results, in Prussia; let us take its best fruits, without going through the same political process. France has done so.

No one can study the constitution of the United States, without perceiving how powerful an influence the principles of the Petition of Right and the Bill of Rights,—which, with the Magna Charta, form the bible of the English constitution, as Chatham said—exercised in producing that memorable instrument. It was right that the framers paid this regard to those great acts, for the age which produced them must be considered, as to some points of constitutional development, classical.

Hampden brought one of the most momentous points in all constitutional history to an issue, and wagered his property and all for thirty shillings six pence, and his trial for the ship-money must be considered as a more important chapter in British history, than some whole reigns. Let us take him as good authority, how important in the higher politics the principle is, no matter how insignificant its direct operation at the moment may be. Political, like moral importance, depends upon the principle, not the value at issue. Judas was not the better for taking but thirty pieces of silver.

The debates of the framers of the constitution of the United States, on this instrument, are valuable authorities, for, in several respects, their time was a classical age in the history of our constitution.

A period may be classical as to commercial law, but not in other respects.

Here it may be mentioned, that authorities may become very strong in an indirect way, namely, if we find that certain principles are acknowledged, *even though* the person, country, or period to which it belongs, are hostile to the subject matter in general, so that their statement is to be considered as one of the last points of truth, which even they could not deny. If we find a principle of British liberty acknowledged even by a Henry VIII., without his having had a momentary and direct advantage in view, it is a strong authority in favor of it. If we find that even in China, the government of which is perfect absolutism, thoretically founded upon parental authority and filial obligation, the maxim is acknowledged, that 'it is equally criminal in the emperor and the subject to violate the laws,' it is strong authority in showing that the law should be superior to every individual will.

IX. *What motive prompted him?* The necessity of carefully attending to this question, has been shown, in section vii. of this chapter, but it is important to add a few remarks.

In citing authorities, it is but too often forgotten, that individuals, as well as periods, however distinguished for certain principles or courses of action, have their phases, to which we must direct discriminate attention, lest we be misled in a very disastrous manner. Lord Coke is very staunch authority on many points, but not when, in 4 Inst. p. 65, he advocates the star-chamber in round terms, and calls it 'the most honorable court in the christian world, the parliament excepted.' Coke, when he drew up the petition of right, was in a very different phase from the one he appears in when prosecuting Essex or Raleigh, or when he endeavored to reestablish himself in court favor by marrying his daughter to a brother of Buckingham. Lord Bacon is a very excellent authority on some points, but not when willing to rack Peccham, which he knew was against law, or when he shamelessly attacked his benefactor

Essex, or when he makes a distinction between betraying justice for bribes, and merely promoting justice for bribes by dispatching cases. Chief Justice Hale is a very excellent authority on some points, but not as to the justice and expediency of trying and punishing witches.

To be brief, nothing is more important in law, politics, history, bellelettres, or any branch whatever, in which we acknowledge authorities—and more or less we must acknowledge them in all—than clearly to present to our minds the peculiar provinces in which we admit them, and then only to admit them if no particular and sufficient reason obliges us to exclude them. On the other hand, if we are fully convinced that a period, or individual, is classical, in the forementioned meaning of the term, on some certain points, it is not sufficient to disregard them merely because we cannot at once see their reasons. We must have specific reasons to discard them; for the idea that they are classical, is that then there existed peculiarly favorable circumstances to decide the point, or to form their judgment, which we cannot at will reproduce. And in decisions on all important matters, much depends upon a certain instinctive feeling, not derived from any course of reasoning, an inclination of our mind one way or the other, in nicely balanced cases, not from whim, but in consequence of long experience, and the effect of a thousand details on our mind, which details, although properly affecting a sound mind, can nevertheless not be strictly summed up. That expression, 'depend upon it, it will turn out so or so,' is very frequently used by those who have no reason in their vacant minds to assign for their opinion, yet it is also of great importance if pronounced by men who do have much experience and a sound mind. Almost every council of war affords instances of this kind. The great general very often knows that a manœuvre will turn out so or so, but, in many cases, he cannot prove it mathematically. A man like Pitt acquires a tact in government measures, and even in matters of law and right, which are very nearly balanced, so much so, that those who have not a long experience in these matters, cannot come to a conclusion, the tact of a Marshal, an instinct, if the word be preferred, may choose the right side. I repeat it, this tact or instinct is not depending upon arbitrary preference, or whimsical choice—if so, it is totally to be abhorred, but it is the effect of long experience in many detailed cases, of practice, upon a mind originally of peculiar fitness for the respective branch in which the important case arises.

If we find that Grecian architects always ornament their architrave with eighteen drops, we may depend upon it that their unequalled sense of the beautiful induced them to adopt this number, and its distribution in three rows, as the only ones which harmonized with the whole character of the fabric, and, unless we discover that there were reasons for adopting this number which do no longer exist, we would act presumptuously in deviating from it, if we adopt otherwise their whole style.

Laws are, in a certain respect, authorities. They have been adopted for some reason or other, and the rule just stated applies to them. It is not sufficient that we do not see at once their use, to abolish them, we must see their positive defects over-balancing their good, or that it be possible to obtain the same good by other means, without incurring the same disadvantages, before we alter them. Otherwise each individual constitutes himself a judge in all matters, as being wise and expert in all branches, which is impossible.

X. *What internal evidence has the authority?* That we ought not to disregard this point any more in the criticism of authorities in law and politics, than in history or any branch whatever, is sufficiently clear. If an opinion from the very highest and most respected source should bear evidence, in itself, that it was given upon faulty principles, we are bound, of course, to discard it at once, for instance, Hale on witch trials, as already mentioned. For this reason, among so many others, all equally strong, it is necessary that we should apply to authorities,

CHAPTER VIII.—SECTION XI. 239

what was found so necessary a principle in precedents, that each case must necessarily be taken with all its adjuncts. It is necessary to understand their very language, for otherwise we cannot give to the words their full meaning, and for this reason, again, authorities must be taken with the more caution, the more remote they are from us, unless they come from a classical age, and we do not live in one respecting the point at issue. 'The modern reports, and the latest of the modern, are the most useful, because they contain the last, and it is to be presumed, the most correct exposition of the law,' says Chancellor Kent. It might be added, because they relate to cases applying to the same circumstances and conditions with our own; they speak the same language with ourselves.

XI. *Of what extent is the authority?* That this is a question of the highest moment in politics and law, appears at once, if we consider that both are matters of experience, not indeed of expediency —I hope I shall not be so radically misunderstood— but of experience that is of sound rules derived by reflecting minds, from the operation of those means to which men have resorted in applying the principles of right and justice to existing cases, or those measures which have most promoted their development or security. If we see that the plan of dividing the legislative department into two branches, or chambers, is almost universally adopted by the constitutional nations of our race, and that the more constitutional law becomes understood, the more it is cherished, it affords good authority for adopting it, even if the people have not yet had a chance to try it, or cannot precisely yet see the admirable operation of this principle, far more important in so called popular governments than even in others, and the Belgians acted right in adopting it, whatever even a Franklin may have said to the contrary. If the independence of the judiciary is daily more and more acknowledged by constitutional nations, it forms good authority in favor of it. Here, as in all cases, we must be convinced, of course, that others act on the same primary principles which we may have acknowledged as essentially important. Else our rule might be made to work in favor of persecuting heretics, whipping soldiers, disallowing counsel to criminally indicted persons, leaving the mass of the people without schools, imprisoning accused and sentenced people pell-mell. We must be convinced that those who have adopted the measure in question, act with us on the same principles, or on principles we acknowledge as good, and that with them the measure is neither the consequence of chance nor the effect of sinister motives, but carefully adopted or developed on those principles.